Sex and Sexuality

Questions and Answers for
Counsellors and Therapists

For Brian
Whose constant love and support
made this book possible

and

Darren, Sarah and Liz
Don't you just hate it when
your mum talks about sex!

Sex and Sexuality

Questions and Answers for Counsellors and Therapists

By

GLYN HUDSON-ALLEZ PHD, CPSYCHOL

BPS Chartered Psychologist; UKCP Registered Psychosexual Therapist;
Director, Association of Counsellors & Psychotherapists in Primary
Care (CPC); Training Manager, British Association for Sexual
& Relationship Therapy (BASRT)

Series Editor
MICHAEL JACOBS

W
WHURR PUBLISHERS
LONDON AND PHILADELPHIA

Contents

female than male, and sometimes think he is neither one nor the other. Can you help me understand the physical and psychological issues involved here?

Chapter 4   **34**

Sexual issues for women

Chapter 5   **51**

Sexual issues for men

Chapter 6   **65**

Sex and relationships

Chapter 7

Discussing sex in the consulting room

Foreword

If there is one area in the training of counsellors and psychotherapists that gets short measure it's the subject of sex and sexuality. This has been the case for more years than I can remember, and there seems little evidence that this has changed. There is no doubt that attention has been paid to improve curricula. Training courses now include the study of the impact of sexual abuse, sexual orientation and even deviant behaviour in our society, but what seems still to be missing is help for practitioners, who need to be able to work with and value the whole of their client's experience, including their sexuality – in other words, common human sexual behaviour.

I have always believed that the most important quality that any counsellor or therapist can offer clients when talking about sexual concerns is their own comfort with the material. This doesn't come naturally for most of us and won't improve if we duck the subject. If counsellors and therapists want to be fully available to their clients, this is the book to assist that process.

Through the medium of commonly asked questions, Glyn Hudson-Allez offers a clear and wise guide, which is both informative and thought provoking. She does not invite the reader to think they need the skills of a psychosexual therapist to engage in exploring sexual material but rather suggests that it is possible to have a normal conversation and that clients may feel mightily relieved to do so.

The questions asked are ones that practitioners will recognize as the ones they wanted to ask but maybe didn't dare. The answers are here and easily accessible. Dr Hudson-Allez has brought her years of experience together and produced a work that manages to offer accurate information while at the same time expanding our understanding of the human sexual condition. This is not another book about sexual problems but one that sets out to have real practical relevance to enhance counsellors' work with clients. As such it should become essential reading for all counsellors and psychotherapists.

Marj Thorburn MBE
Chair of the Professional Standards Board of the
British Association of Sexual and Relationship Therapy 2005

CHAPTER 1
Introduction

When I first trained as a counsellor in the late seventies and early eighties, counselling courses were not as formal and structured as they are today. Much of the learning was done via supervision, peer review and personal reading. In those days, there was very little to read regarding normal sexual activity. Of course, there were seminal works on sexual behaviour, like Kinsey et al. (1948, 1953), Masters and Johnson (1966), Hite (1976), Rosen and Rosen (1981), Apfelbaum (1983) and Bancroft (1989), but these were considered speciality texts for sex therapists and not necessary reading for a general counsellor. When reading counselling texts, if it was mentioned, sex was usually related to Freudian theories that essentially focused on male supremacy and female subjugation. But discussion of what people did, how they enjoyed themselves and whether they could make it better was not part of the accepted texts.

When I reflect back to those days, sex was rarely mentioned in any depth, even in seminars. We were taught the PLISSIT model (Annon, 1976) of allowing clients the permission to discuss their sexual difficulties (see Question 7.1), but there was little movement on from that first stage. We could not even give limited information about sex, because the assumption was made that we should take such knowledge from our own behaviour. If we were respectable people in a heterosexual marriage, it was assumed that we had the requisite knowledge to impart. Homosexuality at that time was illegal, and any form of deviation from 'normal' vaginal penetrative sexual intercourse in the missionary position was considered to need specialist attention. Yet in the counselling room, we would receive questions like 'How much masturbation is too much?', 'How often do other people make love?' and 'Why can't I have an orgasm with my husband when I can have one on my own?' Without specifically going on to train as a sex therapist, this kind of information eluded us counsellors. I found exactly the same avoidance when I later did my psychology degrees.

When Pfizer first started conducting clinical trials on their new drug sildenafil, later to be called Viagra, there was a huge interest in the press that bordered on hysteria. Headlines in the tabloid press like 'PILL FOR IMPOTENCE OUTSELLS PROZAC' shouted the outrage that men (and even, dare I say it, women) wanted to take the drug not just to cure erectile insufficiency but also to enhance their sexual performance. How dare they want to enjoy themselves, possibly at the nation's expense, cried the indignant civil servants in Whitehall! The Government hurriedly put forward prescribing criteria to prevent GPs prescribing Viagra for erectile dysfunction (ED), unless the man had one of a discrete list of physical illnesses, thereby limiting the potential expense to the purse of the NHS. And, even if they were given prescription help to enhance their erections, the patients may have been given only one dose for a week. Similar rationing of sexual activity by GPs was found in the prescribing of Caverject injections; and, if you messed up your weekly injection, that was the end of your sexual enjoyment until the next week. Thus GPs became the gatekeepers to many patients' recreational sexual activity.

The success of Viagra, which was interestingly the unexpected side effect of researching drugs for cardiac problems, was to produce another side effect. It gave British men, hitherto notorious for their inability to speak about things emotional or sexual, the permission to speak openly about sex. As celebrities publicly confessed to struggling to achieve erections when they wanted to, and their willingness to try Viagra, the ordinary man in the street became more willing to say that he had trouble too. I was working in primary care at the time, and I remember that the incidence of clients coming to speak about sexual difficulties increased threefold. Furthermore, as the demand for sexual information, sexual counselling and sexual psychotherapy increased, the number of training places available for health professionals to undertake courses in psychosexual therapy halved. Many valued training courses accredited by the British Association of Sexual and Relationship Therapy (BASRT) and the Institute of Psychosexual Medicine (IPM) disappeared, not because there was a lack of demand for the places but for financial reasons in the training institutions.

With the number of suitably trained psychosexual therapists, or sexologists, dwindling, the knowledge that other health professionals, like counsellors, psychotherapists or psychologists, had to offer was vital. One would have assumed therefore that counselling training, now structured with fixed curricula, would fill the gap. But this does not appear to be the case. In a polemic published in a counselling journal, Clarkson (2003: 9) argued:

> . . . my research work over the last couple of years has proved to me that the literature on sexuality in the fields of counselling, psychology and psychotherapy is (a) conspicuous by its absence (b) factually wrong (c) focused on disorder and dysfunction – negative psychology – and (d) often plainly destructive and damaging.

This is an extreme view, but in the training of health professionals (GPs included) there is a paucity of training about normal functioning sexual behaviour. GPs may only have one or two seminars in their medical training regarding human sexuality, yet, when couples find their sexual activity is not working, their GP is usually the first person they turn to. In my experience of working alongside GPs, although there are some that take an interest in sexual difficulties, there are some who are deeply embarrassed when a patient raises a sexual issue, and there are others who feel they have neither the time nor the interest in getting involved in what may be considered as their patient's recreational behaviour.

Of course, the lack of input on sexuality on training courses for the health professional merely reflects a similar lack of input in British society. The lack of appropriate sex education is an example, as parents predominantly abrogate responsibility for this, for whatever reason, to the schools. Provision of a few classes here or there is inadequate to give children the knowledge and skills that adolescents require when their hormones drive them to start practising a sexual repertoire. There are few schools that provide consistent and repeated classes about sex, and not just about the mechanics of reproduction and the pragmatics of contraception but the physiological understanding of why the person's body is responding the way it does, how to enjoy and stimulate your own arousal systems and how to determine whether one's relationship is appropriate to consummate. Even writing this, I anticipate objections regarding teaching adolescents how to enjoy their own bodies as asking for trouble. Yet it is only by giving adolescents appropriate knowledge about themselves that are they able to make informed choices before sharing in the experience with others.

As a normal part of sex therapy, we undertake a full sexual and developmental history. It never ceases to amaze me how little real education people have had about sex, and how misinformed couples are. This is especially so in heterosexual relationships, where men and women have little knowledge and understanding of how their own body works and tend always to use this information (and sometimes misinformation) to expect their partner to work in the same way. Although there are some similarities between the sexes, their differences, especially in sexual arousal and enjoyment, are greater. Some of this misinformation is not trivial either. I have seen couples struggling to conceive who did not realize that the anal intercourse they enjoyed would not lead to pregnancy. I have seen many men who did not know that women do not urinate via their vagina. These were not ignorant people, but ordinary working- or middle-class folk who had fumbled their way through their relationships and wondered why sex was not as exciting as others made it out to be.

Yet things have changed since my initial counselling training. Twenty years on, clients in the counselling room are much more open to asking questions about sexual activity and sexual variation. This is because it is impossible to read newspapers or magazines, or watch the television, without coming across someone commenting on how people should enhance their sex life. Since I trained as a sex therapist, I am regularly contacted by journalists writing for glossy magazines looking for salacious stories to tap the interests of their readers. Some of them have been really bizarre, like, 'Can you suggest 15 different sexual positions, one for each day to the run up to Christmas?' (My answer was, 'No.') The problem about this, however, is that it gives their readers unrealistic expectations regarding sexual activity. Instead of informing the reader with basic and accurate information, (for example the average man ejaculates within three minutes of vaginal entry), they take what Margolis (2004) calls 'an alphabet-soup' approach to 'finding your G-spot, U-spot or X-spot that will heighten orgasm to the nth-degree'. What this has meant is that questions from clients within the counselling room have become much more specific, and enhanced sexual performance has become a demand to be met rather than a pleasurable extra. Clients will often bring copies of similar articles that they have read in magazines or have downloaded from the Internet, along with their reluctant and embarrassed partner, with the question 'Why can't he or she do this or make me feel like that?'

This book aims to bridge the gap between the specialized psychosexual therapist and the generic counsellor. It offers knowledge and understanding of normal sexual activity to help the counsellor have the confidence to move on with his or her client, from giving permission to talk about sex, through offering limited information, into sometimes making specific suggestions. It is not designed to replace the psychosexual therapist, but it is designed to enhance the skills of the health professional. The format of the book, like others in this series, takes questions that have been raised by counsellors following their work with their clients. Each chapter is divided into themes, as many of the questions and answers are interrelated. Chapter 2 looks at questions involving the differences between biological sex and gender, with discussion about the classic bipolar construction of gender, and whether concepts of male or female are helpful, especially when the client's gender presentation and biological sex may not match. Chapter 3 is concerned with the relationship between body and mind, looking at the developmental progression from infancy to old age and how sexual practices influence both the physical and the psychological worlds of the individual. Chapters 4 and 5 focus on specific presenting difficulties of women and men respectively. Although male and female problems have been divided in this way, it is as well to consider that in any relationship, whether heterosexual or homosexual, the person presenting the 'problem' is merely manifesting the issue on behalf of the couple dynamic, examined in chapter 6. In chapter 7, I address questions focusing on discussing sex in

the counselling room, especially looking at the introduction of the counsellor's   sexuality   in   the   phenomena   called   transference   and
countertransference. Finally, chapters 8 and 9 focus on the variations and
diversities of the perceived stereotypical norm of a heterosexual couple
making love in the missionary position. Even though two chapters are
devoted to these differences, they only cover the tip of the iceberg of the
multiplicity of sexual behaviours that the inventive human being has introduced to make his or her sexual behaviour more interesting and more fun.

CHAPTER 2

Questions of gender

2.1 I am never quite sure what the technical difference is between the terms 'sex', 'sexuality' and 'gender', and which to use when with clients. What is the difference?

The terms 'sex' and 'gender' are frequently confused. Sex is the term used to describe one's biological determination as either male or female, following the confirmation at birth (usually by doctors) after examination of the genitalia, although it may not be as simple as that, as the external genitalia in some people may be ambiguous or may change at puberty (see Question 8.8).

Gender is complex and multifaceted and comprises five elements:

- gender identity
- gender roles
- gender presentation
- gender experiences
- biological sex

Gender identity is a person's self-determination of how they perceive themselves to be masculine, feminine or androgynous. A person's gender identity is thought to have developed by the age of three, and is very much encouraged by parental behaviour. Money (1986) proposes that gender identity is laid down in a 'lovemap' between the ages of three and eight. This lovemap is a developmental representation or template laid out in the brain that will dictate gender and sexuality determinants, and so the child will develop a healthy heterosexual lovemap formation, as long as their development is not vandalized in any way.

Gender identity is based within the brain and is considered to be stable. Gender swings can occur in childhood and adolescence, but rarely in adults. Gender identity may not necessarily be in accord with the individual's biological sex or visible genitalia. Thus some people brought up as women experience themselves as men, some men experience themselves as women and some people have no sense of gender at all. If this experience causes distress, this is called 'gender dysphoria', and they may want to be reassigned from male to female (M2F) or female to male (F2M). These people are called transgenderists (see Questions 8.5 and 8.6). The process of reassignment does not change the gender identity of individuals but brings their biological sex more in line with it.

Gender Identity Disorder (GID) is defined by the DSM IV (1994) as having two components: a strong and persistent cross-gender identification, and a persistent discomfort with his or her own sex. There needs to be evidence of significant distress or impaired sexual functioning. The DSM notes that the incidence of referral between boys and girls is 5: 1, although this may reflect a greater stigma for male cross-dressing (see Question 2.2).

Despite the concept of the 'norm' of a man or a woman, there are a vast number of individuals who, for one reason or another, do not feel comfortable with either description. Thus it may be preferable, rather than considering gender to be a bipolar concept, to consider it as a continuum, that people may move along at various stages of their lives. It should also be pointed out, however, that even the language of 'transgender' implies a bipolar construction of gender, as does the language of 'inter' or 'between' in 'intersex'. As Zandvliet (2000) argues, all categories have exceptions and boundaries, and, where there are boundaries, there will always be people who want to cross them.

Gender roles are the social constructions that are placed upon men and women with expectations that they are required to fulfil the roles according to whether the person is male or female. Contemporary feminism has worked hard to eliminate many of these roles, arguing that women and men should be equal in status and roles should be interchangeable. However, there are still some professions where one gender predominates. For example, the construction industry is predominantly male, although there are an increasing number of women site agents and quantity surveyors. However, the sight of a female construction labourer operating a pneumatic drill is extremely rare. Similarly, men are moving into hitherto female caring professions like nursing, but it is still very unusual to see a male children's nursery nurse or nanny.

Gender presentation is about the way mannerisms, behaviour and appearance conform to biological sex and gender roles. Society has expectations of how men and women should present themselves, although, again, feminism has worked hard to break down some of these barriers. So women in the UK can now acceptably wear trouser suits and men can wear make-up and jewellery, but we have not moved on sufficiently to accept men wearing dresses or skirts to work (even men in kilts would get some flack), although we would accept Middle Eastern men doing so. However, in Thailand, some young boys take on the gender presentation of dancing girls and adopt feminine clothes and appearance that make them almost indistinguishable from the girls.

Gender experiences are the experiences of life that make people essentially male or female, for example a woman's experience of menstruation or childbirth, or a man's experience of penile erection and penetration. These are very gender-specific; thus women who cannot conceive or men who are impotent may experience strong feelings of failure that tap into their gender identity.

Biological sex is determined by external and internal reproductive organs, chromosomes, hormones and gonads. The majority of people have a consistency among these that determine an unequivocal gender. However, a minority have variations and incongruity, for example some people are born with male hormones and female chromosomes.

It can be seen that the concepts of gender and sex are easily confused as the former encapsulates the latter. Both sex and gender are about the individual.

Sexuality, or sexual orientation, is different from gender, as it refers to the emotional and sexual desires for others, rather than people's feelings about themselves. The term describes how an individual displays and interacts with another to form an intimate or sexual alliance. Just as society conveniently assigns a bipolar model on sex and gender as either male or female, there is a similar bipolar model assigned to sexuality, as either heterosexual or homosexual. The human brain stores a vast array of information by developing schemata as a form of categorizing chunks of information (Fiske and Taylor, 1991). These schemata can perform a disservice, however, when we categorize individuals in social interaction in a way that leads to stereotyping and consequent prejudice. As therapists, we need to acknowledge that humans are too complex to fit neatly into two boxes, and, as can be seen in Chapter 8, there are many variations to the concept of sexuality.

When working with clients, it is best not to make assumptions about sex, sexuality or gender based on the appearance or presentation of the client but to use the information and the language presented by the client. And, if unsure, it is possible to ask the client what their gender identity is and what issues this presents for them. Each client needs to be approached as an individual, thus avoiding the natural schematic tendency to place the client into a category.

* * *

2.2   I work with young people, some of whom get called ' tomboy', 'sissy' or 'poofter'. Does that mean they have difficulties with their own gender?

In the answer to Question 2.1, the notion of schemata was introduced to identify the concept of groups or categories in social perception and social interaction. These categories allow our brains to formulate ideas and belief systems in an efficient manner when we meet someone new in order to give us the material required for our social exchange. In doing so, however, we tend to overclassify, and this can lead to stereotyping and prejudice. The terms 'tomboy', 'sissy' and 'butch' are slang categorizations for identifying people who may be seen by others as outside of their gender presentation. Thus the terms 'tomboy' or 'butch' may be applied to a child of female sex who would prefer to climb trees or play football rather than assuming the stereotypical passive role anticipated for girls' play. Similarly, the term 'sissy' may be applied to a boy who is passive and who would rather read, or who may enjoy girls' company, rather than engaging in the stereotypical boys' behaviour of rough and tumble. Interestingly, it has been argued in the feminist literature (Fausto-Sterling, 1992) that it is considered preferable to achieve the label of 'tomboy' than 'sissy', as for a girl to be called a tomboy is considered an increase in social status, whereas for a boy to be called a sissy constitutes a reduction in status.

These stereotypical classifications also apply to sexuality. Thus terms like 'poofter' or 'dyke' are applied to those who are perceived to veer outside the norms of heterosexual behaviour. These terms originally arose as an expression of social control. Individuals who were considered to behave outside of social mores raised anxieties in others, so that name-calling was a means of expressing these anxieties, with the aim of trying to persuade the transgressor back into socially acceptable behaviour. Such terms have now become pejorative as our society has become more tolerant to difference and advocates equal opportunities and political correctness. But the desire to classify, and the desire to use the heterosexual model, is still pervasive within Western societies. This becomes apparent when outsiders observe a gay or lesbian couple and ask, 'Who is the wife, and who is the husband?' It is as if the inability to classify, the actual acknowledgement of ambiguity per se, is anxiety provoking. Being able to assign these roles to same-sex couples, therefore, is reassuring to the perceiver as it fits into a more comfortable frame of reference. The consequence, however, is that sexuality is confused with gender role and preconceived ideas and frames take precedence.

Bem (1975) argues that high sex-role stereotypes are psychologically unhealthy for an individual, and that it is preferable for an individual to demonstrate behaviours from both sexes, or androgynous behaviour, which will allow the person freedom to engage in whichever behaviour is appropriate for the context. She found in her experiments that highly feminine females were correlated with high anxiety and poor social adjustment scores and were less independent. She does not argue, however, that society should be composed of androgynous individuals. Her point is that society should stop being schematic in assigning people and behaviours stereotypical roles.

This question asks whether children who are labelled by others with these terms have issues with their gender. In short, the answer is no. They are simply behaving in a way that feels right for them in the expression of their own personality. Indeed, it could be argued that it is more likely that it is the individuals who are assigning the names in the first place who have the problem, as they are too bipolar and rigid in their thinking styles. Nevertheless, children (and adults) who experience such prejudice may well be scarred by it.

* * *

2.3   I feel very uncomfortable when I work with couples where the men want to assert their dominance over their female partners, insisting that 'she' should stay at home and look after the children, as this goes against my own beliefs. Aren't such gender roles old-fashioned?

Gender roles are a social construction, and not necessarily an aspect of an individual's biological sex. The stereotypical roles of men going to work and being the bread-winner, while women stay at home and care for the man and the children is a typically Western phenomenon that is not necessarily mapped out in other cultures. For example, the North American Indians have an ancient tradition of gender role-swapping, where some women join hunting parties and some men take on the child-rearing role. The crossing from one gender role to the other has been considered acceptable in this type of society; it involved long periods of preparation followed by an initiation ceremony as the person moved from one role to another. This was named by Europeans as 'Berdache' from the Persian word *berdaj*, a pejorative term to describe a passive homosexual partner, usually a pretty boy. Yet the North American Indians were not threatened by these individuals and were completely accepting of this 'third gender'. Berdache men often became healers, doctors, therapists or priests, or became one of the multiple wives of an Indian brave and would be viewed by the tribe as having mystic and psychic qualities.

Gender roles are thought to be constructed from learned behaviour. Through observational learning and imitation, a child takes on the role demonstrated by the same sex parent, which is reinforced by the verbal and non-verbal feedback from the parent to the child. Smith (1978) conducted research by observing how adults interacted with infants, according to whether they were dressed in pink or blue irrespective of the biological sex of the infant. Those dressed in blue were stimulated and encouraged to be active, were bounced around, lifted up in the air and were given toy hammers to shake and bang. Those dressed in pink were pacified, soothed, expected to lie still and were given soft toys to cuddle. There are many studies that have demonstrated how such stereotypical gender roles are reinforced throughout infancy and early childhood.

From a psychodynamic perspective, the traditional gender-role identification was developed through the Oedipal period of development (Freud, 1901). Children needed to be brought up with a strong, authoritarian father and a caring, nurturing mother. A male child would feel his father to be a rival for his mother's love but also be aware that his father is strong and powerful. By aligning himself with his father and acting in the same way, he protected himself from any direct threat. It has been argued that if this process did not occur the child would become homosexual, particularly if the child were brought up with a weak father and a strong and dominant mother. However, research has not validated this theory. Golombok et al. (1983) undertook a study comparing children raised in lesbian families with children raised in traditional heterosexual families and found no differences in the children's gender identity, gender-role behaviours or sexual orientation.

The counsellor in this question is expressing discomfort with the client's belief system, and it may be producing a countertransference reaction that relates to his or her own history. It may be that this discomfort should be examined in supervision. However, countertransference reactions may also provide valuable information on what is happening within the couple. Perhaps the man's real feelings are ambivalent, but he is mirroring the only role that he knows or is comfortable with. Or perhaps a useful piece of work would be to encourage the female to be more assertive and find the voice to express what her views are.

* * *

2.4   The feminist revolution has shown us that women are capable of doing the same things as men given a similar set of circumstances, and I take great care in the counselling room to approach my clients without a gender bias. However, am I right to suppose that men and women approach love and sex in the same way, or are men really from Mars and women from Venus?

My opinion, which may differ from some feminist thinking, is that we ignore differences between men and women at our peril, especially when undertaking therapy with them. In term of sex issues, I believe we can identify:

- differences in love
- differences in sexual drive
- differences in arousal
- differences in fertility

There are other differences, but here I concentrate upon these four aspects.

Differences in love: The psychological literature proposes that there are six kinds of love (Lee, 1973):

1. **Eros**: romantic love, focusing on physical attractiveness and sensuality
2. **Ludus**: game-playing love, no commitment and not to be taken seriously
3. **Storge**: friendship love based on caring not passion
4. **Pragma**: pragmatism on a cost-benefit analysis
5. **Mania**: possessive, dependent love (co-dependency)
6. **Agape**: selfless and compassionate love as preached by Ghandi, Buddha or Jesus (and as such very rare)

Research shows, against contemporary belief, that men tend to be romantics (eros), as well as game-players (ludus) and are more likely to develop an obsessive desire for possession (mania). Women, alternatively, are more likely to be pragmatic, with a lesser element of mania (Hendrick et al., 1984). Walster and Walster (1978) agree that men fall in love earlier than women and are more romantic in their views of love, whereas women are more pragmatic, with over two-thirds of a research sample saying they would marry a man whom they did not love if everything else about the person was acceptable (see also Kephart, 1967). Research has also shown that women who are in love are more likely to fall out of love sooner than men. So men are called FILOs (first in, last out) and women are called LIFOs (last in, first out) (Duck, 1986).

Differences in sexual drive: Kaplan (1995) divides sexual drive into six levels:

1. hyperactive sexual desire – sexual addiction, Don Juanism
2. high-normal sexual desire
3. low-normal sexual desire
4. mild hypoactive sexual desire
5. severe hypoactive sexual desire
6. sexual aversion disorder – sexual phobia

This is a useful spectrum that corrects the idea that sexual desire is a unitary concept, although I prefer to include a level between 2 and 3 that might be described as 'average' (as opposed to 'normal': what, after all, is 'normal'?). However, more recently Riley (1998) has proposed that men and women's normal levels of desire are skewed distributions on the opposite ends of the normal range, with the majority of women at the lower end and the majority of men at the higher end, with the exceptions forming the tails of this distribution (see Fig. 2.1). This means that there

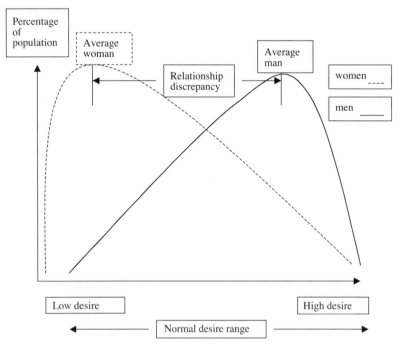

Figure 2.1 The differences in sexual arousal between men and women, after Riley (1998).

will tend to be a discrepancy between the frequencies they will want to make love, and that most men will tend to want to do it more often than most women. The consequence of this fundamental difference is that if a woman always allows sex when the man wants it, and does so before she is ready, it becomes a less satisfying experience and makes her less willing to want to repeat it. This discrepancy in sexual arousal is dealt with more fully in Question 6.3.

Differences in arousal: Men and women are also different in the way the body becomes sexually aroused. Men have a natural visual feedback loop, which allows them to see their own arousal, which taps directly into their cognitive process of sexual desire. Women, however, do not have such a visual pathway, and they may not necessarily be able to access feelings of somatic arousal. Thus their cognitive pathways are essential to their getting themselves aroused and ready for sex, as Kaplan (1995) says, 'priming the pump'. Women tend to be more responsively sexual, rather than spontaneously sexual (Goldmeir, 2001), and they seem to have cognitive pathways to follow:

1. This person is making advances to me. Do I find this person desirable/acceptable (pragmatic) to be sexual with?
2. If yes, can I be bothered? (Am I too tired? Stressed? Have the children been playing me up? Have you helped with the chores? Have you been nice to me?)
3. If yes, I will allow you to arouse me (responsive).

Thus, women have to go through a cognitive process to determine whether they are willing, or can be bothered, to be sexual before their body starts to respond. Because of this, it takes them a great deal longer to become physiologically aroused and needs their active cognitive consent.

It might therefore be said that for women foreplay begins at breakfast. As part of her cognitive process, her partner needs to be nice to her all day. There is no point in his (or her) coming home from work at the end of a tiring and stressful day, snarling at her, shouting at the kids, kicking the cat, then expecting her to be up for sex at bedtime. She will think, 'No way, José!' Men tend to overestimate how long they allow for foreplay to get a woman responsively aroused, and it is a frequent complaint from women that 'he has finished before I have even started'. However, men are between a rock and a hard place, because very often women do not tell the man where she is in her arousal process, but expects him to know. If he takes too long, she gets irritated and might think, 'For goodness sake, get on with it!' If he is too quick, she accuses him of being only out for himself and not really interested in her, hence the importance of communication between couples.

Women are trained from birth to be multitasked, which means focusing on sex and sex alone can be hard work, and some even find it boring. Most women expect a sharing relationship, which includes sharing domestic chores. Domestic slaves do not feel sexy. She also wants to communicate with her partner and tell him her problems. Unfortunately, most men are problem-solvers and want to offer solutions to her problems, whereas she just wants someone to listen. What then might follow is the thought 'If you can't listen to me, I don't want to be sexual with you', and sexual arousal shuts down.

Differences in fertility: Men can be fertile (although this can depend on their levels of smoking, drinking, eating etc.) from puberty to death. Women, however, are only fertile from puberty to menopause, and for one week out of every four-week cycle; and their post-menopausal years may equal their fertile years. Thus, biologically speaking, women are having sex more when they cannot conceive, and, once they have produced their offspring, they have less investment in being sexual; especially post-menopausally. Nature makes up for this discrepancy by allowing women to have repetitive orgasms to make it more interesting for her, whereas men have a refractory period before they can have sex again – going from ten minutes if he is eighteen years old, to a week or so if he is eighty. Some post-menopausal women feel they have to stay on hormone replacement therapy (HRT) to delay their menopause in order to keep their partner interested, because they fear he will search for a younger, sexually active partner if they lose interest in sex.

Of course, there are other differences between men and women. Men tend to express love through sex; thus, when a woman does not want to have sex, he may feel personally rejected. Women express their love through the relationship and in the way they care, with sex being an optional, and generally less intrinsically important, extra. Women do not necessarily want to have an orgasm every time they have sex either and may become irritated by a man who insists she is orgasmic, or even multi-orgasmic, as if otherwise she is not getting the most out of her sexual experience. Similarly, she may not be always interested in penetrative sex but may prefer other activities. One of the most useful educative tasks of the therapist is to help such men to realize that they are expecting their women to respond to sex as a man does, rather than as a woman.

* * *

2.5   I am seeing a male client who tells me he was born with a minuscule penis. He is somewhat feminine in some of his mannerisms too. I sometimes wonder whether he is more female than male, and sometimes think he is neither one nor the other. Can you help me understand the physical and psychological issues involved here?

The factors that determine an individual's biological sex comprise:

- their internal and external genitalia
- their chromosomes
- their hormones
- their gonads

Each individual has a pair of *sex chromosomes* that helps determine their biological sex. Every foetus derives one chromosome from their mother, which is the X chromosome. The other chromosome comes from the father, and this may be either X or Y. Females have two X chromosomes, whereas males have one X and one Y (named because of their shape under a microscope). This Y chromosome is thought to be the reason for some sex-linked disorders that occur more in men than in women, such as colour blindness or haemophilia. We also know that the presence of a single Y chromosome, no matter how small, will produce testes.

The *gonads* are the reproductive organs, which are the ovaries in women and the testes in men. There are also hormonal differences between men and women that affect sexual characteristics. Male hormones are called androgens, such as testosterone, which is released by the testes. Dihydrotestosterone (DHT) is the hormone that provides men with their masculine appearance. Impaired androgen synthesis, or failure to make sufficient testosterone, will give an outward feminine appearance, and is medically called an 'undervirilized male'. Deficiencies in the androgen system can lead to various problems, such as congenital adrenal hyperplasia, leading to intersex problems (see Question 8.8). The literature suggests a range of prevalence of such syndromes between three and seventeen in one thousand live births. Only about one-third are picked up at birth, usually via hernia investigations. The rest manifest in puberty and may be offered surgical, fertility and/or HRT options. For further discussion of this aspect see Questions 2.1 and 8.8.

The most important female hormones are oestrogen and progesterone, both produced by the ovaries. However, both men and women produce all the hormones, although the differential is greater in the relevant sex. For example, if a female has excessive secretion of androgens by the adrenal gland or gonad during critical stages of development, this will cause virilization of the female.

For the client with a micropenis and feminine mannerisms, it may well be that he has an androgen deficiency and may be considered an under-virilized male. However, there is no reason, even if that is the case, that he cannot have successful and satisfactory heterosexual relationships if he is anatomically and physically normal in structure. The brain is the main sexual organ and an androgenized brain will push men in a male direction. It would be helpful for the counsellor to help the man explore these issues to find out what underpins his sense of inadequacy. A discussion around the spectrum of gender, as opposed to a bipolar concept (see Question 2.1), may also help him to accept himself as 'normal' and lift his self-esteem. It may also be helpful to be able to acknowledge that it is not the size of the penis that is important in making him a man; it is the experience of himself as masculine or feminine. Correspondingly, it is not the size of a male partner's penis that is important to his female partner but how he uses it.

CHAPTER 3

Body and mind

3.1 I am seeing a client who is expecting a baby boy. She and her partner cannot agree whether or not the boy should be circumcised. What are the advantages or difficulties the boy might have when he grows up if he is circumcised?

Circumcision is the partial or complete removal of the prepuce, or fore-skin, from the penis. In some religions this is a requisite procedure for male infants, although it was originally introduced into Western culture in an attempt to reduce masturbatory practices. It is a controversial proce-dure as it is mainly carried out without anaesthesia because this can be dangerous in young infants. An infant therefore experiences the full pain of a surgical procedure, which removes approximately one third of the penile system, without pain relief. The removal of the appropriate amount of foreskin during the procedure is vital. Too little, and the parents are like-ly to return the child for a further procedure. Too much, and the child may experience painful erections when adult and a curvature of the penis.

It is often held that a circumcised penis is cleaner and more hygienic. However, this implies that the 82% of men who have not been circumcised have unhygienic penises, and this is certainly not the case. It is also a myth that a circumcised penis is less likely to contract sexually transmitted dis-eases or penile cancer. Thus, the majority of circumcisions are carried out for religious or cosmetic reasons. Removal of the foreskin may prevent problems later in life, as some men find that their foreskin is too tight, does not retract sufficiently over the glans of the penis and as a consequence causes pain and discomfort during sexual intercourse, although this hap-pens to less than 1% of the male population.

The removal of the foreskin has its problems. Some infants have experi-enced repeated infections as a result of the procedure due to faecal matter within the nappy infecting the surgical site. These infections can lead to meatal stenosis, where the opening of the urethral tract narrows to prevent sufficient urination. Scar tissue can also build up and may require later corrective surgery. Some men, on obtaining adulthood, have sought to have foreskin restoration procedures. And some infants, because of a slip of the hand at the time of the circumcision procedure, have had their whole penis accidentally removed. Money and Tucker (1975) recount the story of an infant to whom this happened. The doctors decided to remove the testicles as well, and the parents reared the child as a female. It was held during childhood that this was a wholly successful procedure and she was said to be a feminine child. During adolescence, she was required to have oestrogen injections for breast development. Rebellion took place when she reached fourteen years of age, however, and began to live as a boy. As an adult, he had a double mastectomy, had reconstructive surgery for a penis and scrotum and later married and adopted children (Diamond, 1979).

As the couple in this question cannot agree to circumcision, it may be helpful for them to obtain knowledge of the various procedures from their local hospital. In addition, there are videos that can be obtained so that the parents can be clear about what is involved. It would be helpful to explore with the couple what it is that underpins their disagreement. Does one of the couple want the circumcision for religious reasons, but the other partner does not share this view? It would also be valuable to ascertain the couple's knowledge base, in case one of the couple is holding a myth regarding the advantages or disadvantages of circumcision. If, when the whole situation has been explored, and agreement still cannot be reached, would a compromise be to allow the child to grow until he reaches an age when he can make the decision for himself?

* * *

3.2 A parent I am working with is worried that her five-year-old son is very interested in sex. She thinks he should not show such interest at this age. How might I help her assess whether his interest is normal or whether there may indeed be some sexual issues around?

Contemporary parents in Western society would have us believe that right up to the age of sixteen, a child is completely innocent of sexual interest or desire. There is a paradox of adults openly displaying their sexual potential in newspapers, in advertisements, on television and in films, while at the same time encouraging the idea that children can be kept completely untouched by this and retain their child-like innocence until after their sixteenth birthday. Indeed, following the latest Sexual Offences Act 2003, it is now a criminal offence to have a sexually explicit communication with a child under the age of sixteen unless you are a health worker and are not actively causing or encouraging that child to be sexual. In this case, the counsellor is required to inform the child that any sex he or she undertakes is illegal.

When Freud (1901) proposed his theory of child development, which focused on a child's developing sexuality, there was a similar expression of outrage by Victorian society. Yet Freud developed his theory based on the observation of his own children. Although modern psychology has moved away from much of Freudian theory, there is one thing that is clear to objective observers: children are inherently sexual and practise their sexual potential, particularly with their opposite-sex parent. For most children this is a safe frame in which to learn about the dynamics of relationships and sexuality. Unfortunately for some children, the parent is unable to hold the boundary to allow it to be a safe frame.

Freud proposed that children went through a series of stages in their development:

1. *oral stage*: birth to 12 months – the focus on sucking and gratification through the mouth
2. *anal stage*: 1 to 3 years – focusing on potty training and learning control, and gratification through urination and defecation
3. *phallic stage*: 3 to 5 or 6 years – developing an interest in one's own, and others' genitals ('You show me yours, and I'll show you mine' stage)

He also proposed an Oedipal stage – where the child needs to resolve the conflict of loving the opposite-sex parent and seeing the same-sex parent as a rival, although he proposed a slightly different resolution of the Oedipus complex for boys and girls.

4. *latency*: 5 or 6 years to puberty – a stage of putting sexuality to one side in order to focus more on educative and physical tasks
5. *genital stage*: puberty to adolescence – learning and practising sexual behaviour

While this theory has a lot to commend it, it does have some basic flaws in its assumptions. An in-depth analysis of Freudian theories is not appropriate in this text; however, the theory does make some assumptions that do not hold true with modern society. For example, it implies that a child needs both a male and a female parent in order to develop in a balanced way. Yet modern society, with its high divorce rate together with a substantial number of people choosing not to marry, has a large proportion of single parents bringing up children without the ongoing support of both a male and female carer. In addition, there are an increasing number of same-sex partnerships bringing up their own offspring. What is becoming clear is that these children are not sexually dysfunctional but are able to develop deep and meaningful relationships with others outside the family unit, providing they do not receive negative or inappropriate messages within it.

The client mentioned in this question is the parent of a five-year-old who is expressing, according to the parent, too much interest in sex. It may be useful to know whether the child is expressing interest in sex or genitals. As already mentioned, the child in this question may well be in the 'bums and willies' phase of genital interest, and it is quite normal to see a little boy of such an age squatting down trying to look up the skirt of a mannequin in a shop window, curious about what lies underneath, or for a young girl sitting on a man's knee to ask, 'Have you got a willie?'

However, the child may be rather more than curious or knowledgeable about sexual behaviour, which would raise more serious concerns about what he may already know or have been introduced to. Careful questioning, without jumping to conclusions, is vital in this situation. We know that abused children have knowledge before their years as they are introduced to a sexual repertoire before they have the necessary sexual drive to put it into action. But it may equally be that this child has inadvertently intruded upon his parents having sex or maybe shares the same bedroom with them.

Also, it is worth checking about the child's own level of physical sexual development. Modern children are reaching puberty at much earlier ages than those of previous generations. There is also a condition called precocious puberty (the youngest mother recorded giving birth was aged five) in which the child's hormones activate too soon, leaving such a person with the body of a woman (or man) yet the emotional and intellectual development of a child.

Finally, it is worth establishing whether the mother's anxieties about the child's behaviour are really about the child or whether she is revisiting her own childhood abuse issues.

* * *

3.3 Working with adolescents, I am never sure whether there is an age when a boy or girl is too young to have sex. I know there is a legal limit, which is often ignored, but is there any place for concern about this?

Part of normal human development is the development of sexual potential at puberty. For a girl it will be the development of small breasts following the emergence of nipple-buds, pubic hair, changes in the muscle structure of the body and the start of the menstrual cycle. For boys, it will be the breaking of the voice, development of muscle structure, growth of body hair and enlargement of the penis and scrotum. Both girls and boys will indulge in auto-erotic behaviour at this stage, and, rather than discouraging them at this time, a balanced approach is to accept that it is normal behaviour which nearly everyone does in privacy, and is fine providing they treat themselves and others with respect. Children, probably from the age of eleven onwards, are going to indulge in sexual exploration, both with themselves and with others. It is a sexual rehearsal for being adult.

The legal enforcement of sexual behaviour is difficult to conceptualize. It is designed to protect children from abusive and predatory adults, who for their own gratification want to move children into a sexual repertoire before they are ready. So an arbitrary age delineation is made. In this country the age of consent is sixteen years, even though most children will have had some form of sexual experience before reaching that age.

As previously mentioned in Question 3.2, the Sexual Offences Act 2003 makes it an offence to have 'explicit communications with children about sex'. This was designed to prohibit the grooming of children into sexual behaviour via the Internet. However, as a by-product, it could have put psychosexual therapists, counsellors, family-planning advisors, teachers and even doctors at risk of prosecution if children brought sexual concerns to them to be discussed. As a consequence of this concern, a defence has been introduced to cover health professionals who are providing sexual education or sexual health advice 'as long as they do not cause or encourage the child's sexual activity'.

Counsellors working with adolescents also need to consider Gillick competency. In this legal ruling, parental rights yield to the child's right to make his or her own decisions regarding treatment when he or she reaches a sufficient understanding to be capable of making up his or her own mind on the matter requiring decision. Thus, a young person (fortunately the Law Lords chose not to put an arbitrary age delineation on this) who is considered to have sufficient knowledge and understanding to give consent to treatment, including counselling, is considered Gillick competent. However, the Gillick ruling has already been amended, now called the Fraser Guidelines, following Lord Fraser's ruling that every attempt should be made to persuade the child to involve the parents. However, if the child still refuses, the child's wishes may prevail.

If an adolescent shares with a counsellor that he or she is sexually active, and that activity is fully consensual with no element of coercion, maintaining an objective, non-judgemental stance irrespective of their age is the best approach, as with an adult. If the adolescent insists they have no wish that their parents know about the counselling, and they have sufficient knowledge and understanding regarding the consequences of that decision, the law allows the confidence of the counselling to be kept. However, the Sexual Offences Act requires the counsellor to inform the adolescent that they are breaking the law by engaging in sexual behaviour.

* * *

3.4   A male client is getting frustrated because his partner, who had a baby a month ago, does not want sex with him. Is this usual? How does childbirth affect having sex?

One paradox of loving relationships is that the child created as a consequence of that love can have a divisive effect on the couple. It is considered that 75% of married couples experience severe problems, with 35% of these reporting considering separation within two years of the birth of a child (Ayles and Reynolds, 2001). For approximately 40-70% of couples there is a drop in marital quality and conflict increases by a factor of nine (Pacey, 2004). The most common reason given for this is lack of sexual activity either during pregnancy or during the child's early years. Women vary in their response to pregnancy and childbirth, sometimes influenced by their own experiences as children. Usually, the woman experiences an increase in sexual interest during the first and second trimester of pregnancy and then a gradual decline in the third (Bing and Coleman, 1977). Ganem (2004) found that couples who remained sexually active into the eighth month of pregnancy had less problems between them after delivery. Benefits found were less likelihood of post-natal depression, easier initiation of sexual intercourse, a shorter gap before resuming sexual intercourse and better communication between the couple regarding the nurturing of the baby.

Robson et al. (1981) undertook a study of women and found that two-thirds resumed sexual activity between the sixth and twelfth week after delivery, although sexual frequency dropped considerably, and a year later about 20% were having sex less than once a week. Predominantly, the reason for this lack of sexual activity after the birth is the mother's decline in sexual interest (Bancroft, 1989) and tiredness. After the euphoria of the birth initially dies down, the mother settles into a routine where the little one demands her attention, both day and night. Mother becomes too exhausted to want to be physically active; when she goes to bed, all she wants to do is sleep while she has the chance. As her sexual arousal commences at a cognitive level (see Question 2.4), she is likely to switch off any arousal system until she has more time and energy. It is also thought that women release the neuropeptide vasopressin as well as oxytocin during breast-feeding, both of which are linked to the powerful protective feelings of parenting, but in doing so may underpin a woman's loss of interest in sex (Hillier, 2004). Pain during intercourse as a result of birth trauma and episiotomy scars are likely to be another factor, as is a loss of body image if the figure is not regained. There may also be the fear of a repeat pregnancy. In addition, some women become very anxious at the responsibility a first baby brings. Motherhood requires acquiring new skills, the same as any other new task.

The male client in this question says he is frustrated at his wife's lack of interest in sex. However, in addition to exploring the issues mentioned above, it may be useful to consider the dynamic between the couple, especially if the child born is their first child. As the wife becomes involved with the infant, some husbands feel isolated and abandoned from lack of attention or even jealous of his wife's love for another individual. In addition, breast-feeding can become a mutually enjoyable and time-consuming pastime for mother and infant, but from which father is excluded. Indeed, he may have previously considered that his wife's breasts were his domain, from which he has been usurped. Thus, supporting the couple while they discuss their hopes and fears regarding the addition to their family might help to unpack the dynamics of their changed relationship. Encouraging them to make time for each other as well as the infant may also assist them, as will enlisting the help and support of extended family and friends. As the woman progressively feels secure as a result of the intimacy in the relationship, her sexual interest is likely to return.

* * *

3.5   A male client has asked me how he finds his girlfriend's G-spot. Is it factual information he wants or could there be other aspects to his question?

The G-spot takes its name from Ernst Gräfenberg, who discussed the potential erogenous zone in the 1950s (Gräfenberg, 1950), but it was not popularized until the 1980s when a book called *The G-Spot* was published (Ladas, Whipple et al., 1982). It is thought to be an area on the anterior wall of the vagina, about one finger's length along, through which, with firm pressure, one can feel the paraurethral or Skene's gland. Likened to the female equivalent of the prostate, it was argued that stimulation of the gland increased its size, like the clitoris and labia, and can produce such an intense orgasm that she releases a discharge of fluid, often called the female ejaculation. The popular press took hold of this idea, and numerous women's magazines advocated that it was essential that women have a G-spot orgasm. This has led to many women feeling inadequate, either because they cannot find the G-spot or they fail to have the intense orgasm proposed.

There are many misconceptions about the G-spot. First, it is not a scientific fact that it exists. Second, there is a great deal of controversy regarding female ejaculation. Some say it is a version of prostatic fluid, others that it is vaginal lubrication, others that it is urine. Most likely it is combination of all of these. Third, the G-spot is not a spot but more of an area or zone. And fourth, some women will find other parts of the vagina more erogenous than others. There are always individual differences. The biggest problem with the issue, however, is that some women are led to believe that stimulation of the G-Spot is the only way for them to have an orgasm. This means that, for the considerable proportion of women who cannot find one, they may feel lacking or that they are missing out.

The male client in this question says that he cannot find his girlfriend's G-spot. He probably holds misconceptions about it from the media and therefore needs factual information. However, it is also necessary to determine the reason for his question. Does he feel his girlfriend is not getting sufficiently aroused? Or does she, like nearly 50% of women, fail to achieve orgasm through penetrative sex? Or does he just want to take her to ecstatic heights she has hitherto not reached? Whichever the case for this client, it would be well worth his establishing what *her* views are on the subject!

* * *

3.6 I am seeing a client who was depressed but is much better now, but he is still not interested in sex. He is still taking antidepressants. Could they be affecting his sexuality?

One of the symptoms of depression is a loss of libido. Indeed, it is one of the first symptoms to appear in a depressive state, and one of the last symptoms to leave on recovery. Some research studies have suggested that up to 90% of people being treated with antidepressants, particularly Specific Serotonin Reuptake Inhibitors (SSRIs), have an iatrogenic, or drug-related, sexual dysfunction; the most common complaints are erectile dysfunction (ED), retarded ejaculation (RE) and anorgasmia. The effects of SSRIs on sexual functioning seem strongly dose-related and may vary among the group according to serotonin and dopamine re-uptake mechanisms, and propensity for accumulation over time (Hudson-Allez and Robertson, 2003). Together with the loss of libido of the depressive state anyway, sexual dysfunction while on any form of antidepressant should be considered highly likely.

Some people with depression are seriously concerned about the sexual effects of their treatment. Unfortunately, the recommendation for taking antidepressants is that the patient continues to take them for six months after becoming asymptomatic of the depression. This can be a considerable period of time in having a drug-induced dysfunction, which can be very distressing and may be very detrimental to a couple in an already unstable relationship. Interestingly, women are less likely to report sexual side effects of treatment to their doctor and are more likely to adopt sexual avoidance strategies within their relationship.

Although the effective treatment of depression should be the overriding concern, sexual dysfunction may be an important problem to the depressed patient and may contribute to the maintenance of the depressed state. Although it is not appropriate to counsel the person to cease their medication too soon in order to regain their sexual functioning, there are some SSRIs, like mirtazpine (Zispin), that are less likely to induce sexual problems. We know from the outcome literature that there is little to choose between the efficacy of one SSRI and another, but there are differences in each side-effect profile. This client might therefore be encouraged to discuss with their prescribing GP or psychiatrist a change of SSRI. Meanwhile, the counsellor can usefully work with the client in helping him resolve the underlying issues of the depression, which, of course, may be added to by his concern about sexual potency.

* * *

3.7   I have a number of older clients who have anxiety about their sexual performance and wonder if it is to do with their age. What physical changes for men and women occur with ageing? And how might I respond to their anxiety?

Ageing affects both men and women sexually, but that does not mean they need to cease having enjoyable sexual activity with their partners. The media can lead people to have unrealistic expectations about sex and a couple's activities, which in turn lead many older couples to believe that sex is an activity for the young. But this need not be the case so long as the couple are realistic regarding their expectations.

In the Massachusetts male-ageing study, Feldman et al. (1994) found that over 50% of men questioned between the ages of forty and seventy years had experienced erectile dysfunction (ED) at some stage in their lives, and 10% were completely impotent. Similarly, Holmes et al. (1997) estimated the incidence of ED as 5% among men in their forties, 10% of men in their sixties, 20% in their seventies, 30–40% in their eighties and over 50% for men in their nineties. Thus, there is an expectation that, as man becomes older, his erections may fail or be less solid. This finding is linked to a reduction in the frequency of sexual intercourse in later life. Pfeiffer (1974) conducted a study as to why couples ceased sexual activity in their middle years and found the most common reason given by men ceasing to be sexually active was their own inability to perform. As can be seen in the answer to Question 5.2, this no longer need be such a difficult issue as there are many interventions currently available to help a man with a failing erection.

Another reason for the reduction in the frequency of sex as a man becomes older is that the refractory period, the time a man has to wait before being able to have sexual intercourse again, becomes much longer. Thus, a young man can have an ejaculation several times within a few hours. However, this would not be usual in an older man, and the older he gets, the longer he has to wait. There may also be a decline in his level of circulating testosterone that helps to maintain sexual activity. Riley (1988) found that men who were widowed and thus had a break in their sexual activity were subsequently likely to have erectile problems. He argued that the break in sexual activity could have caused a degeneration in the hormonal system. And finally, as men get older, they may also suffer with physiological problems that may affect their ability to be sexual: such problems might be prostate enlargement, diabetes, vascular degeneration, hypertension etc. Thus, the ability to achieve an erection as and when one wants, as occurred when a young man, becomes a myth for the older male.

For women, changes will occur first after childbirth and latterly after menopause, and these are discussed in more detail in the answer to Question 4.8. However, menopause does not have to herald the ending of fulfilling sexual relations. Many women at this time feel liberated from the monthly period and the need for contraception. They are more likely to be able to express their sexual wants and needs to their partners and are more likely to say that sex is better than it was when they were younger (Starr and Weiner, 1981).

The reduction of female hormones at menopause leads to a reduction in lubrication, atrophy of the vaginal barrel and a thinning of the vaginal walls. Thus penetrative sex may become dry and painful. Question 4.6 discusses the issue of painful sex, or dyspareunia.

Older clients may feel anxious regarding discussing their sexual activity with an outsider, especially if the counsellor is considerably younger. There may be the perception that the counsellor would disapprove or suggest that it is inappropriate. The client may also have grown up in a generation where people were not encouraged to discuss their sexual behaviour and that the activity should be kept private. Croft (1982) writes about the myths of sexuality and ageing, including:

- coital satisfaction decreases after menopause
- older men lose their ability and desire to have sex
- older people or those with physical disabilities should not engage in sexual activity

It is useful for a counsellor to introduce some of these myths into the discussion with the client as a way of drawing out other myths that the client may hold. A frank discussion, together with information-giving, can allay a lot of anxiety. Gibson (1992) also points out that counsellors should have fully examined their own belief system regarding the sexuality of older people. He points out that, if an older woman discusses applying for cosmetic surgery and HRT in order to get a 'toy-boy', the countertransference may be to that of the counsellor's own parent and so produce a negative response in the counsellor. It is essential, therefore, that the counsellor can stay with the client's own wants and needs, irrespective of their personal views.

* * *

3.8   I am not sure what I think about anal stimulation and anal sex when clients talk about it. Is it a substitute for genital sex, as I think Freud said, or is it OK? What if the partner objects?

Freud discussed the anus as an erogenous zone and as a strong focus of pleasure that people could enjoy throughout their life. However, Freud's Victorian view of sex was that the only appropriate form of sexual activity was vaginal intercourse, thus anal stimulation per se was, in his view, immature and simply one step in foreplay on the way to genital intercourse.

As is discussed in Question 8.4, anal intercourse as a normal aspect of human behaviour can be traced back to the ancient Greeks. It was considered at that time essential for a well-educated boy to receive anal intercourse from his teacher, as it imparted knowledge, wisdom and respectability (Morin, 1998). However, over the years, views have changed, and many countries have established anti-sodomy laws. Thus the concept of the anus becoming an erogenous zone has been lost to vast sectors of the world's population until recent times when the gay liberation movement became politically vocal. Yet even though it was an international taboo that people did not discuss, anal sex was something that many people were prepared to engage in, in the privacy of their own relationships. Peterson (1983) found from a survey of 100,000 readers of *Playboy* magazine that 13% of married couples practised anal intercourse more than once a month and 63% had engaged in other forms of anal stimulation. Thus anal intercourse is not just the province of gay men.

The anus has two sphincters that surround the anal opening. These are in direct contact with the perineal muscles, which support the muscles between the anus and the genitals. When sufficiently relaxed, the anal muscles and the anal canal are capable of vast expansion, sufficient to take a person's complete hand and even part of the forearm (fisting). The two sphincters, which slightly overlap, can then close to return the anal orifice to its usual size. Although not a common activity in relationships, fisting does happen and those who practise it feel very close as it requires a great deal of trust and giving in the relationship for it to occur. Most couples are content with the insertion of fingers, penises or penile-shaped objects, or aids like vibrators for anal and rectal stimulation. If the couple concerned are gay men, they may choose to engage in anal intercourse, although many do not and prefer mutual masturbation. If the relationship is a man and a woman, anal sex may be chosen as an addition to vaginal intercourse or sometimes to replace it, for example if there is fear regarding conception.

Problems may occur in relationships when one partner wants to engage in an activity and the other objects; this situation is common both with anal and oral sex. If one of the couple is reluctant to engage in anal stimulation, it may be helpful to encourage elaboration on the basis of such objections. Frequently, the underlying emotion is fear. It may be due to fear of encountering faeces, fear of pain, of not being able to do it correctly or of feeling inadequate. No one should insist that their partner engage in a sexual activity if they are reluctant or ambivalent, as it will lead to the destruction of mutual trust and respect. However, by openly sharing fears and concerns, and sensitive understanding on behalf of the partner, the fear and reluctance may be attenuated, especially if the counsellor encourages some form of quid pro quo agreement. The counsellor could also suggest the reluctant partner experience anal stimulation under his or her own control, by using small dilators and small vibrators to allow the person to experience the arousal of anal stimulation before moving on to letting someone else do it for them.

* * *

3.9 I am seeing a client who has developed herpes but insists she has not had any sexual partner other than her husband. What advice should I give her regarding having sex in the future?

Genital infection with the herpes simplex virus usually causes multiple painful ulcers in the region of the genitals, buttocks, anus and thighs. In women the ulcers may develop on or around the vulva, inside the vagina and on the cervix. The first infection occurs after a short incubation period of seven days after infection and starts with red patches (erythema), which blister, ulcerate and then crust. If the ulcers coalesce, there can be substantial pain and discomfort, especially with urination. Clients may complain of pain in the groin as well as at the ulcerated sites, constipation and discharge. Some people will also become lethargic and feverish.

Herpes is a disease transmitted by oral or sexual contact. It is possible for the type 1 strand of the herpes simplex virus, facial sores (cold sores), to be transferred to the genitals via orogenital contact. The type 2 strand of herpes, genital herpes, is transmitted via sexual intercourse. Herpes is an unpleasant, recurrent illness for which there is no curative treatment, although recurrent infections tend to be less severe than the primary attack. Herpes can also be passed on to infants during childbirth.

The client in this question states that she has had no other sexual partner other than her husband. It is therefore likely that she contracted the infection from him, and he should therefore attend a genito-urinary clinic for assessment and treatment. It may be that he is one of a group of people who have the virus and are asymptomatic or whose symptoms have been so minor that they have not been attributed to herpes. It is possible therefore that he has had the infection for many years and not been aware of it. It is equally possible that her husband has had a sexual relationship with a third party and recently contracted the infection from that person.

The client needs very careful emotional support at this time, and it is essential for the protection of the relationship that conclusions are not drawn without sufficient evidence. Clients need to be advised of the risk of sexual behaviour while they are experiencing a viral attack, and that a condom may be insufficient to protect a partner from contracting the virus. If the client is a woman of child-bearing age, there needs to be a discussion around the risks to any future infant. The client is likely to undergo a grieving process for the loss of her health in contracting a lifelong, incurable and unpleasant disease. There may also be mourning for the loss of fidelity within the relationship, if this is the case. Self-esteem will also be an issue as the client's perception of herself as tarnished may ensue, and there may be myths about never being able to form a new relationship, becoming infertile or developing cervical cancer, all of which need to be frankly discussed.

* * *

3.10 I am seeing a client who had a one-night stand of unprotected sex two years ago, and has been fearful ever since that she may have contracted HIV. Her fear is so intense that she has dismissed the idea of having a test as she is terrified of a positive result. How should we work through this?

HIV (Human Immunodeficiency Virus) is the causative agent of Acquired Immune Deficiency Syndrome (AIDS), a fatal illness with no curative treatment. The virus is transmitted through sexual contact, bodily fluids and perinatally. About two to six months after infection, seroconversion takes place, and may be accompanied by a fever, malaise and a rash, similar to glandular fever or meningoencephalitis (ME). Following infection there is a delay of three to six months before antibodies can be detected. The individual is predominantly asymptomatic during this time and may be so for many years. Others develop a series of minor recurrent infections. The development from HIV to AIDS is thought to take eleven years, and from AIDS to death, three years (Sonnex, 1996).

The client in this question is a woman terrified that she has contracted HIV from a casual sexual encounter without protection. Her fear is such that she is frozen into inaction in case she learns that she has contracted the virus. In this situation, some factual information-giving may help remove the paralysis from her fear. In the UK, 92% of those who contract the HIV virus are men, and of those women who do contract the virus the majority are intravenous drug misusers or women who have had sex with intravenous drug misusers or a bisexual (Weller, 1995). Thus, the chances of her contracting HIV are low, whereas the chances of her contracting another sexually transmitted disease like chlamydia is much higher. It has now been two years since her casual encounter; so, if she had contracted the virus, the antibodies would be well established by now. Therefore a test will tell her; but taking the test may have implications in other areas of her life, for example with insurance or mortgage companies. It may be, with this in mind, inappropriate for her to take one on the basis of a one-night stand and no physical symptoms.

The focus of the work in this case would be more fruitful if it moves away from the aspect of HIV, which colludes with the client's excessive rumination. The client's value system, or that of her family of origin, may have been so outraged by her own risky behaviour that she has moved into a form of persecutory self-flagellation by her intrusive and obsessive thoughts. Spending time working through why she is punishing herself in this way, or whether she is acting out how another (for example a parent) would punish her, might help put her fears into perspective.

* * *

3.11 I undertake domiciliary counselling for a woman who has been bed-bound for half her life. We have discussed her normal sexual desires, but she dismisses the idea as she has no strength for personal pleasuring and feels it is too embarrassing to have to ask one of her carers for an aid. How can I help her with this?

In a society that values beauty and bodily perfection so highly, people with disabilities are not only handicapped by their disability; in addition they are handicapped by other people's perceptions of them (Hudson-Allez, 1994) and this also influences how they may view their own bodies. In the answer to Question 3.7, I discussed the myth that sex should only be for the young. In this case, the myth extends to suggest that sex is only for the able-bodied and physically lithe. Historically, people with physical disabilities were kept in an asexual state with only their basic nutritional and hygiene needs met. Sexual needs would not be a topic for discussion with carers. For those with a cognitive disability, however, there was an active focus to prohibit any form of sexual activity, often through the use of psychotropic medication and enforced sterilization in case they reproduced children with similar imperfections.

Taleporos and McCabe (2003) conducted a large survey of people with disabilities to determine whether they were likely to form relationships, the extent of their self-esteem and their sexual behaviour. They found that the more severe an individual perceived their own disability to be, the less likely they were to be in a relationship. A high need for assistance with living as a consequence of the disability was correlated with being single. The severity of the disability may limit the individual's willingness to enter into intimate relationships, but there is also a limit to social situations in which the person can enter in order to meet a potential partner, which in turn limits their social skills. Issues around body image, pain in certain positions, fears regarding continence or poor coordination may also be inhibitors. And for many of the bed-bound, the genital area becomes purely a place to be cleaned and wiped, not stimulated and aroused.

It is positive that the counsellor in this question has already discussed the client's normal sexual desires with her. Raising the issue is essential when working with people with disabilities, as they may become conditioned to shutting their sexual feelings down and feel it a subject that is not open for discussion. It is not clear what disability the client in this question experiences, but she clearly feels that she is too weak to masturbate and too embarrassed to ask a carer for a sex aid. It may be that this woman was never encouraged by her family to consider her sexual needs, may not have been educated to understand them or may have grown up in an overprotected environment and has been treated as asexual all her life (Bass and Davies, 1988). It may also be that this client's hand is not sufficiently strong enough to hold a vibrator. However, it is now possible to purchase vibrators that slip over the end of the finger and therefore need no strength to hold. Thus, together with a good lubricant, the client may be able to experience some pleasurable bodily sensations rather than fatigue and pain. There are also special beds that are divided up into large sections of differing heights and widths which can be placed together to allow the person to lie unaided in position to enhance sexual activity, either with themselves or with another.

It is difficult for a person who never leaves their bed and is therefore reliant on others to provide for their needs to undertake behaviour that for the rest of us is essentially a private activity. Such a person may feel as if they are living in a goldfish bowl, with someone observing their every move. But well-trained carers understand the importance of sensual and sexual stimulation for people with disabilities, the same as it is for everyone else, and can provide them with the tools to be sexual, and then provide them with the privacy to be so.

CHAPTER 4
Sexual issues for women

4.1   What sexual problems that women may have can I work with as a therapist, and what sexual problems should I refer elsewhere?

I might begin by asking a question myself: Do women have sexual problems and does female sexual dysfunction (FSD) exist? According to an article in the *British Medical Journal*, it is argued that FSD is a medical disorder classified purely by drug companies racing to develop new drugs to enhance the sexual activity of women (Moynihan, 2003). Moynihan argues that cited prevalence rates of FSD of 43% are exaggerated and that the drug companies are constructing the condition; that difficulties become dysfunctions that become diseases.

The article created huge controversy and a plethora of responses on the Internet; some agreed with the notion that sexual dysfunction has become operationalized as a marketing tool for the pharmaceutical industry. The majority, however, disagreed with Moynihan's viewpoint. For example, Bancroft notes that the inhibition of sexual desire might be a normal, healthy response for women faced with tiredness, stress or threatening patterns of behaviour from their partners. Dionne argues that male-dominated medicine did not accept FSD as a physiological problem but as a psychiatric issue. And Lundquist points out that (male) medics still do not accept that, like men, women have a sexuality of their own which can go wrong, which does not have to be frigidity or the wrong man. Overall, most criticisms pointed out that researchers over the years have systematically ignored women's sexual problems, until Pfizer and other companies tried to search for a female version of Viagra. So in a sense, Moynihan is right in that investigations began post-Viagra, but he is wrong to suggest that hitherto the problem had not existed.

Women are less likely to present with sexual problems than men, and not necessarily because they are more embarrassed about it. It is partly because sex is less important to them overall, partly because they have less of their personal identity wrapped up in their sexual performance and partly that their pragmatism tells them that, even if they do tell their GP that they have gone off sex, the GP will either not be interested or will not be able to offer any remedy.

So when a counsellor discusses relationship issues with a female client, often a difficulty in sexual behaviour will emerge as a related issue. It is helpful here to explore the dynamics of her arousal and desire systems (see Question 2.4) because that will give a clearer insight as to whether she is not being sexual because of something physical as opposed to the psychogenic facets of the relationship or her own sexuality bias. If the former, the most common physical difficulties women experience are:

- impaired sexual interest – loss of drive, loss of desire, lack of arousal
- anorgasmia – inability to achieve an orgasm (see Question 4.5)
- vaginismus – clamping of the pubococcygeus muscle preventing penetration (see Question 4.3)
- dyspareunia – painful sex (see Question 4.6).

All need referral to both a medical doctor and a psychosexual therapist.

* * *

4.2 I recently saw a client who was angry with his girlfriend, saying she was faking orgasms. He knew this because he could not find her clitoris when she was supposed to have been aroused. Is there a way to tell if a woman fakes an orgasm?

There are two parts to this question that need to be clarified: first, the physiological aspect to arousal and clitoral erection in a woman and, second, whether orgasm can be determined by a partner.

Two outer lips, or labia, protect the vulval area of a woman (see Fig 4.1). Inside, two inner labia emerge from the base of the vaginal opening, circumventing the urethral opening and sheltering the external part of the clitoris at the top by a hood-shaped fold. Internally, the clitoris divides into two wing-like structures that wrap two-thirds of the way around the vaginal barrel. These inner components are as different for each woman in shape and structure as is her face. Beneath the urethral opening is the vaginal entrance, which is not a hole but folds of skin that have the potential to stretch into a passageway, as does the anus further below again. The hymen is a fold of skin in the outer portion of the vaginal barrel that occludes the passage but tears with penetrative sex, tampons or vigorous exercise. Between the vagina and the anus, the skin is called the perineum, which is a very sensitive erogenous zone.

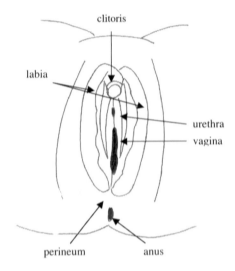

Figure 4.1 The vulva.

When a woman becomes sexually aroused, blood flows to the vulval area engorging the labia, making them increase in size and darken in colour. The outer lips open and the clitoris becomes erect. As the clitoris is erectile tissue, it is highly sensitive, and too much stimulation can become painful, so it protects itself at the peak of arousal by tucking under the clitoral hood. Thus, women are more likely to get highly aroused by teasing around the clitoris than by applying pressure directly on it.

The client in this question says he cannot find his girlfriend's clitoris and therefore assumes she must be faking her orgasms. It may help this client for the counsellor to provide some factual information regarding the structure of a woman's genitalia, as it is likely that the reason he cannot find her erect clitoris is because she has become so aroused that it has tucked itself under the clitoral hood.

The second part of the question relates to whether he can know that his girlfriend is experiencing a real orgasm or is faking it. It may be possible to determine by a change in her breathing or by feeling her muscles contracting around his fingers or penis. But the counsellor might usefully raise the question as to why she would want to fake orgasms. A woman does so either because she wants to stop the penetrative act or she wants to make her partner feel better, and feels under pressure to achieve an orgasm that either she does not want or is not materializing. If she felt that her partner would let her take responsibility for enjoying her own sexuality, instead of being affected by achievement anxiety, she would have no need to fake an orgasm. The onus therefore returns to this client: his keenness for his partner to have a genuine orgasm is the issue and not whether or not she is actually achieving what he so desperately wants her to achieve.

* * *

4.3 I am seeing a woman client who cannot achieve penetrative sex. Should I refer her for specialist help?

A female who cannot achieve penetrative sex may be experiencing a condition called vaginismus. This is the involuntary and often conditioned bodily response where contraction of vaginal, or pubococcygeus, muscles prevent penetration into the vaginal cavity. These women will not be able to tolerate any sort of insertion into the vagina, including tampons or a doctor's speculum for a cervical smear. It has been argued that the current medical emphasis of vaginismus as the woman's ability to be penetrated is inappropriate, rather the focus should be on the women's experience of, or fear of, pain (Ng, 2000) or as a defence against sexual violation. Vaginismus is often the result of some form of vaginal trauma. Jehu (1988) found that 94% of women who were sexually abused as children had some sexual dysfunction. It may also be conditioned from continual medical bowel investigations, for example for Crohn's disease.

Some useful assessment questions for a counsellor to ask a client who experiences vaginismus might be:

- Do attempts at penetration cause pain?
- Where does the pain occur?
- Does the pain occur if the woman is aroused?
- Is she or her partner aware of the muscle spasms?
- Is vaginal penetration ever possible?
- Can she or her partner insert a finger or a tampon?
- Has a doctor's speculum caused the same experience?
- Has she experienced any trauma to do with the vagina?
- Are there any fears about giving birth?

The treatment for vaginismus requires a medical examination first to ensure there are no physical issues that may be overlooked. The counsellor can help the client with learning relaxation therapy. After an exploration of any childhood or traumatic issues, it is useful to explore whether the client actually wants vaginal penetrative sex as a goal. For some women, especially lesbian women, it may not be. If this is what the client wants, however, behavioural therapy with a psychosexual therapist using graded vaginal trainers/fingers or dilators may help her to achieve it.

* * *

4.4   I have a client who had a pregnancy termination. She did not expect to grieve the way she is and has become terrified that she will never be able to conceive again when she is ready to have a child. Is this something that is likely to occur?

As with any medical procedure, termination of pregnancy does have some risks, whether it is conducted by suction in the early stages of pregnancy or by surgical procedures for a more advanced pregnancy. The risks include damage to the cervix, pelvic infections, a higher incidence of future miscarriage and depression. The main risk to the fertility of the woman is that her Fallopian tubes may become infected, leaving them blocked by scarring. This can prevent the eggs moving down the tubes for fertilization. However, for the majority of women, undergoing a termination of pregnancy will not pose a risk to future pregnancies.

Termination of pregnancy has become a common occurrence, and many women believe the myth that because they made the decision not to continue with the pregnancy they will not grieve for the loss of the child. This may be the case with some women, but many do experience grief, especially if the termination is carried out later into the pregnancy. Grief has a depressive aspect to it, which will impede sexual libido after the termination. There may also be psychological factors that will impede sexual desire which are connected to the reasons for the termination, for example if the relationship was casual or unsatisfactory. In addition, libido may be inhibited by a fear of further pregnancies. The counsellor can help this client by focusing on the here-and-now situation that led to the termination, rather than spending too much time focusing on whether the client will be able to conceive in the future.

* * *

4.5 Several female clients I have seen have clitoral orgasms but have never had a vaginal orgasm. As a male counsellor I am not sure I understand whether this is an issue or not, or even if it is an issue if a woman enjoys sex but never has an orgasm. Am I right to be concerned about this?

It is interesting that a male counsellor worries about whether women have clitoral or vaginal orgasms, whereas most women would only worry if they do not have an orgasm at all. So I address lack of orgasm, anorgasmia, first and then return to the issue of vaginal or clitoral orgasms.

Anorgasmia is where a woman has never achieved an orgasm, or only achieved orgasm under rare conditions. It may be that the woman can be orgasmic with herself but not with her partner. This suggests that insufficient clitoral stimulation is occurring, as about half of women are unable to achieve orgasm during penetrative sex. In this sense it is not true anorgasmia but a difficulty that may be due to poor sexual skills on behalf of the partner and inhibition on the part of the woman in being able to communicate that to him or her. Anorgasmia can also be caused by physical problems like diabetes or multiple sclerosis, or iatrogenic causes like medication. Psychological causes for this condition may include the fear of losing control, high levels of inhibition or cultural, religious and/or parental negative messages regarding women's enjoyment of sex. The need to fake orgasms may also demonstrate a form of response anxiety due to the fear of not achieving what her partner expects of her (Schnarch, 1991).

Some useful assessment questions for the counsellor to ask a client who experiences anorgasmia are:

- Does orgasm occur under any circumstances, like masturbation or oral sex?
- Does she get aroused and lubricate?
- Does she receive sufficient stimulation from her partner?
- Does she ever feel close to orgasm?
- Does high arousal invoke anxiety?
- How does she feel an orgasm should be?

This last question is important and leads us on to the second part of the question. There are huge individual differences when women experience orgasm. Some women experience a small flutter of muscle contractions during their orgasm that may well be overlooked. For other women it is a *When Harry met Sally*, full-blown, 'Yes! Yes! Yeeeessss!!!' explosion. Even within the same woman, her orgasms will vary from one time to another.

Thus, expectations play a huge part in what is going to be achieved. These expectations, of course, work the other way, and can lead to fears of losing control, fears of urinary or faecal incontinence or fear of what her face might look like to her partner or of crying out if she really lets herself go.

It was Freud (1901) who wrote that women were biologically inferior to men, and were predominantly suffering from penis envy. He originally wrote about the concept of immature clitoral orgasms experienced by young girls, as opposed to the vaginal orgasms of a mature woman. Thus, if a woman failed to achieve an orgasm as a result of the male-preferred method of penetrative sex, she could be accused of being sexually immature or even infantile. In this respect, Freud's concept has largely been discredited. Victorian women did suffer from penis envy not because of their lack of visible genitals but because of their inferior status and because of the humiliating and demeaning comments that learned men like Freud wrote about them, comments that were largely believed by society as a whole. Margolis (2004) argues that one of the reasons for Freud's assertion may have flowed from a Victorian male vanity and an angry rejection of the idea that a woman could achieve an orgasm and achieve sexual pleasure without the aid of a man.

Freud was right, however, about there being different forms of orgasm for women depending on where the stimulation takes place. A vulval orgasm may occur with clitoral stimulation, and a uterine orgasm may occur from deep vaginal penetration. Modern-day researchers have inevitably increased the pressure by advocating the G-spot orgasm (see Question 3.5), the U-spot orgasm in the sensitive opening of the urethra, the fornix orgasm in the tenting part of the vagina and even the X-spot orgasm on the cervix. All this does is to make an ordinary woman, who is unlikely to distinguish between any of these, feel very inadequate and missing out if she is not able to identify and achieve all of them.

What is important for a counsellor, whether they are male or female, is to be able to convey to a female client that worrying about achieving or not achieving an orgasm is likely to inhibit it anyway. The worry becomes self-fulfilling, whether the worry is that she is oversexed because she wants an orgasm each time she makes love and does not get it or the worry is that she is 'less of woman' because she does not achieve an orgasm every time. Indeed, many women are not bothered about an orgasm on every sexual occasion and are quite content to stop sexual activity whenever their partner climaxes. This is because the neuropeptide oxytocin (see Question 4.11) that she produces during sexual activity has already done its job and made her feel warm and protected and loved. Thus, counselling can help a client decide what she wants for herself rather than feeling pressure from external factors, like the media or her partner, as what she feels she ought to have.

* * *

4.6   I think the sexual problem with the wife of a couple I see may be due to a physical problem, as she experiences real pain with penetration. However, her GP keeps telling her it is all psychological. What should I do?

This client is suffering with dyspareunia, or pain or discomfort during sexual intercourse. There are many physical causes to dyspareunia, like endometriosis, vaginitis, vulval vestibulitis, cystitis, episiotomy scars from childbirth, sexually transmitted diseases, multiple sclerosis, arthritis, diabetes, vaginismus or even an intact hymen. It is therefore essential that the woman be checked out for any of these physical possibilities first. However, there can be psychological causes to dyspareunia, for example trauma in her past, an unhappy or unsatisfactory relationship because she no longer loves her partner or covert homosexual tendencies. The counsellor also needs to check out whether penetrative sex is a goal for this couple (it may not be for lesbian couples). Such psychological difficulties can lead to physical problems with the concomitant lack of sexual arousal and insufficient lubrication for pain-free penetration.

Useful questions for the counsellor to ask a client at assessment for dyspareunia are:

- Does the pain occur at the entrance or deep within the vagina?
- Is it a sharp sting or a dull ache?
- Does she also get pain in her back?
- Does she get pain when passing water? (cystitis)
- Does she have vaginal discharge or itching? (STD)
- Has she been raped or had traumatic childbirth?
- Does she have pain when she is aroused?
- Does the pain only occur during intercourse or does it persist?
- Does she get the pain at any other time?

These questions will aid the client in focusing on the problem and thus aid her GP.

In the case of the wife of this couple, I presume she has been checked out by her GP through a physical examination before declaring the problem is psychological. If a physical examination has not been conducted, she needs to visit another GP for a second opinion, or she could attend her local genito-urinary medicine (GUM) clinic. A client can self-refer to these clinics, where clients are seen anonymously and with sensitivity. If the GP has discounted physical reasons for the pain, it may be as well to check out potential psychological issues. However, it is not clear how old this woman is. Is she post- or peri-menopausal? There might be natural causes for the pain. During menopause, the vaginal wall becomes thinner as it atrophies, and women stop lubricating, making the friction of penetration uncomfortable and sore (see Question 4.9). Recommending a vaginal lubricant, like Sylk or Senselle, may be a simple remedy to a painful problem.

* * *

4.7   A couple came for counselling because they were not having sex. The wife said she wasn't interested in sex and would rather read a good book. The husband said she was not normal and insisted she have treatment. Is it our role to encourage women to be sexual when they have no desire to be?

There are two aspects to this question that need answering:

1. the aspect of impaired sexual interest (hypoactive sexual desire, or HSD)
2. the ethical issue of giving someone sex therapy when they have no wish to be sexual

Women have a large cognitive element to their sexual arousal (see Question 2.4) and can shut down if they feel conditions for being sexual are not right, such as pressure to have sex. As Kaplan (1995) points out:

> The psychogenic form of this syndrome is caused by their active, albeit unconscious, selectively negative cognitive and perceptual processes by means of which they literally 'turn themselves off'. (Kaplan, 1995: 4)

Kaplan suggests that this is an unconscious process. In some cases it may be. But there are also many times when it is a conscious decision that she does not want to spend the time or the energy in being sexual (see Question 2.4). Tiredness, demanding children, anger, mistrust, depression, stress, fear of intimacy, trauma and power struggles in the relationship may all contribute to this problem. Of course, it is not necessarily a conscious or unconscious decision. Hormonal influences may reduce sexual drive as testosterone drops or with the peaks and troughs of the monthly cycle. There may also be iatrogenic causes from psychotropic medication, the pill or HRT.

Some useful assessment questions for the counsellor to ask a client pre-senting with impaired sexual interest are:

- Is there a total or partial loss of interest?
- Does it relate to your partner or is there attraction to someone else?
- Does your partner engage in sufficient foreplay to allow you to become aroused thereby making it a satisfying experience for you?
- Do you have arousing fantasies or daydreams?
- Are there other physical symptoms like loss of energy or depression?
- Are other changes occurring in the relationship?
- Does desire vary with the menstrual cycle?
- Is there any intra-personal sexual activity like masturbation or nocturnal orgasm?

In the assessment it is valuable to assess her for co-morbid conditions, like depression, anxiety, stress or other chronic illnesses. If the problem is not physical and there are no other underlying conditions, psychosexual therapy might help the person get aroused before engaging with her part-ner, using sensate focus, sexual-skills training and erotica.

In Question 4.5, I suggested that some women are less interested in achieving orgasm than their male partners. Leif (1988) points out that many women fail to remember their orgasms and that it is such an unstim-ulating experience that it fails to lead them to want to repeat such an experience again. Indeed, many women prefer the warmth and security of a loving relationship with lots of kisses and hugs but are less interested in the sexual-performance side. However, sometimes their male partners want them to be multi-orgasmic as it demonstrates their own masculine prowess and makes them feel assured that their wife is happy and satisfied. Similarly, the media contribute to the pressures on women when they read glossy magazine articles with titles such as 'Fifteen ways to enhance your daily orgasm'; if this is something they do not achieve, they may feel that they are missing out. This is why Loulan (1984) refers to the 'tyranny of orgasm'. It is also known that one-third of women never achieve sponta-neous sexual desire, even though they can achieve arousal and orgasm when stimulated (Garde and Lunde, 1980).

The second part of this question is an ethical one that raises more ques-tions than it answers. If a woman is content to read a book or to do her knitting rather than wanting to be sexual, should counsellors or therapists try and change that just because it is what her partner wants? Even if she is willing to go through the process of therapy, should the counsellor do so if the woman does not want to be sexual for her own sake but simply because she wants to save a failing relationship? Very often, a psychological sexual dysfunction serves a purpose, and in this example maybe this wife finds her husband overbearing or intrusive. The husband is saying she is 'not nor-mal' and 'insists she have therapy'. This may be a good reason not to undertake therapy with her. He is blaming her and forcing her into a situation that she would rather not be in. But it is also possible that, if a therapist could help her recapture her sexual desire, she might want to be sexual with her partner; thus, is not giving her therapy colluding with her passivity? Careful discussion with the couple over the ethical issues raised, and each partner's motives, may help to answer some of these questions.

* * *

4.8   I am seeing a lesbian couple in a long-term relationship, where one has had a double mastectomy. She is feeling so bad about her body that it is affecting their sexual relationship. How can I help them?

Britain has the highest mortality rate for breast cancer in the world, with one woman in twelve developing the disease (Glanville, 2001). When caught early, however, breast cancer need not be fatal. Bilateral mastectomy (removal of both breasts) and the removal of the lymph nodes is considered to be a valuable (although controversial) method of preventing metastasis into other organs of the body. However, in doing so, mastectomy can have a profound effect on the sexuality, body image and feelings of femininity of the woman. It has therefore been increasingly common for surgeons to undertake breast reconstruction procedures at the same time as undertaking the mastectomy. Cytotoxic and hormonal chemotherapy, which may be a part of the treatment, can also lead to ovarian suppression, vaginal discharge or dryness, dyspareunia and loss of interest in sex (Fallowfield, 2004). Some doctors have prescribed testosterone to women who experience a loss of ovarian function to help them restore their libido. There may also be psychological changes when a person experiences a potentially fatal illness.

For this couple, one woman has had a double mastectomy and is experiencing body dysmorphophobia. It is not clear whether she has had reconstructive surgery, which does help with body image, but some women still struggle to come to terms with the thought of implants and scarring. However, it is likely that the other partner is experiencing some grief for the loss of her partner's breasts too, which even if reconstructed will look and feel different. This partner may feel unable to express this, as it may be considered a minor and insensitive issue compared to the enormity of the partner recovering from a life-threatening illness. Resuming sexual relationships after cancer may be an after-thought with some oncologists, as the primary aim is the preservation of life. It is important, therefore, in follow-up care, that this woman and her partner are able to talk through with their medical professionals any option for helping with sexual difficulties.

Counselling with this couple can help them to overcome the pain of loss in their relationship and to consider how to re-establish intimacy. Encouraging them to touch each other sensually in front of a large mirror using sensate focus techniques can also help desensitize the bodily changes. They need to be able to communicate explicitly to one another about the changes in physical sensations and whether there are any changes in suppleness or stamina. Thus, a new way of being intimate, which may need to be more planned than previously, is a preferable focus for the work rather than trying to recapture what has been lost.

* * *

4.9 What does menopause do to relationships? I seem to have had a number of women clients who have divorced around that period of their life. Does menopause spell the end of a good sex life? Or is it the opposite, that these women want something more?

Women have been told for years that menopause is the end of useful womanhood, that when reproduction ceases, so does their value to society. Wilson and Wilson (1963) blame this 'cow-like negative state' on being oestrogen-starved, and that lack of oestrogen was the reason for alcoholism, drug addiction, divorce and broken homes. Rueben (1969) agrees. He describes a menopausal woman's degeneration in this way:

> The vagina begins to shrivel, the breasts atrophy, sexual desire disappears . . . Increased facial hair, deepening voice, obesity . . . coarsened features, enlargement of the clitoris, and gradual baldness complete the tragic picture. Not really a man but no longer a functional woman, these individuals live in a world of intersex.

How do women prohibit this fate worse than death? Some authorities will say 'HRT (Hormone Replacement Therapy) of course'. Not only will HRT give women their lives back, it will also make huge profit for the pharmaceutical companies!

This approach to menopause has made a normal developmental transition, which for some women may cause unpleasant symptoms for a while, into a disease model that has to be rectified. Doctors have told women that HRT makes sense as it stops osteoporosis, heart disease etc. and allows women to maintain their sexual functioning. What women are not told is that it increases the risk of cancer, that it makes them put on weight and, in some cases, that they will lose their libido. So why has HRT not been the magic pill that everyone expected it to be? The reason is that the search for a drug which focuses purely on replacing oestrogen or progesterone, and in some cases testosterone, takes a reductionist approach to a biological phenomenon that also includes the changing in levels of follicle-stimulating hormone (FSH), luteinizing hormone (LH) and androstenedione. Menopause is not just about the absence of oestrogen but the gradual lowering of availability of ovarian oestrogen (Fausto-Sterling, 1992), and the increase of synthesis of adrenal oestrogen, which levels out following menopause. It is the fine balance between all these hormones that the body is trying to achieve in its attempt to self-regulate. Increasingly, more women are turning away from medical interventions for their normal developmental transition and moving towards using nutritional (Glanville, 1997) and lifestyle methods for dealing with some of the unpleasant symptoms as their bodies re-adjust.

So how does menopause affect relationships? Menopause occurs for most women between their fiftieth and sixtieth birthdays, the mean age being 51. This is already a time of transition for many women as they move into a stage of life when they are no longer tied with children. Far from expecting to suffer with 'empty-nest syndrome' with the loss of offspring, many women experience menopause as a time of release from the scourge of monthly periods and the fear of pregnancy, as well as the freedom without children to do what they want to do. They may have greater disposable income and may choose this part of their life as a time to develop a new career before settling down in a decade hence for retirement. Change is scary for both partners in a relationship, and some men cannot cope with the change that they see in their wives. Similarly, some women, no longer feeling tied by the children, decide that their partners have been insufficiently supportive through the child-rearing years, and, now the children are no longer holding them to this relationship, may choose to move on. But the greater majority of relationships are not damaged by menopause at all, and both partners enjoy the freedom to be together without the children, to go places and do the things that they want to do.

Does menopause change women sexually? We do know that following menopause there are physical changes, as the vaginal walls atrophy and become thinner and lubrication slows down. This can cause the friction in sexual intercourse to be painful. If a woman chooses not to take HRT, either orally or with vaginal creams, there are now many vaginal lubricants that can be purchased, like Sylk, Senselle or Vyelle. Just like any other part of the body, if a woman continues to use her vagina, she is less likely to lose it. Women, because their arousal is more cognitive, vary in their levels of sexual arousal after menopause. Some become more sexually active because they are enjoying life more; others experience a loss through a reduction in their testosterone levels.

* * *

4.10 One of my clients has had a hysterectomy and is now unsure of herself sexually. What are the issues I might need to bear in mind?

It is estimated that hysterectomy is one of the most commonly performed operations in the UK, with over 1,000 being performed each week (Glanville, 2001). A hysterectomy removes the uterus and sometimes other parts of a woman's reproductive system as well (see Figure 4.2). There are six main types:

- total abdominal hysterectomy – removal of the uterus and cervix through the abdominal wall
- total abdominal hysterectomy with bilateral salpingo-oophorectomy – removal of the uterus, cervix, ovaries and Fallopian tubes through the abdominal wall
- sub-total abdominal hysterectomy – only the uterus is removed and the cervix is left intact
- vaginal hysterectomy – the uterus and the cervix are removed through the vagina
- laparoscopically assisted vaginal hysterectomy – keyhole surgery through the abdomen to release the uterus and cervix to allow removal through the vagina
- radical hysterectomy – removal of the uterus, cervix, Fallopian tubes, the upper portions of the vagina and pelvic lymph nodes

How do any of these procedures affect a woman's sexuality? Any hysterectomy that includes oophorectomy procedures plunges the post-operative woman into an instantaneous menopausal condition. This may have a negative effect on her libido. Some studies suggest that the removal of the cervix interferes with orgasms as a result of damage to the nerve endings in the uterovaginal plexus (Hasson, 1993). For women who have had a part of their vagina removed, they may request a vaginoplasty if the resumption of penetrative sex is their goal, although some say that vaginal sensations are diminished after hysterectomy. A loss of oestrogen may

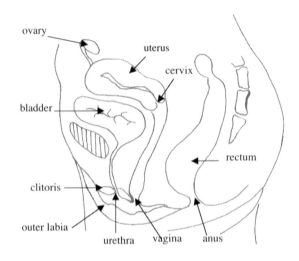

Figure 4.2 The female pelvic organs.

also cause vaginal dryness and any subsequent sex painful. However, many women find after the three months of convalescing from a hysterectomy that they are more willing to be sexual, as it frees them from the difficulties of fibroids and heavy periods, endometriosis, chronic pelvic pain, prolapse or pre-cancerous conditions that originally caused them to have the hysterectomy. It was the pre-operative condition that had reduced their willingness to be sexually active and when they were less likely to experience orgasm. Some studies therefore suggest that the sexual relationships of women are enhanced after a hysterectomy (Rhodes et al., 1999).

The client in this question is unsure about herself sexually following her hysterectomy. The extent of her surgical procedure or whether she is in a relationship currently is unclear. However, the counsellor can help her talk through her anxieties regarding the procedure. She may have feelings of a loss around her womanhood and her ability to bear children. She may have body-image issues if she had an abdominal procedure and has been left scarred. The surgical incisions may have cut through nerve endings, and so she may find she has reduced sensation in the cervix and vagina. However, a hysterectomy does not seem to impair the sensitivity of the clitoris, and so her ability to achieve orgasm should be unimpaired. The counsellor can encourage her to re-explore her own body again, to find what sensations she can now enjoy before sharing this with her partner.

* * *

4.11 One client I am seeing was telling me that she had lost her libido. During the session, I was shocked to discover that, as is usual in her culture, she had been genitally mutilated. I know nothing of such practices other than that they are illegal in this country. Would this procedure account for her loss of desire?

Female genital mutilation (FGM) has been a practice in many cultures for thousands of years. It was developed by the men within the culture who were fearful of their women's potential for sexuality; so it was designed to distinguish the pure woman from the prostitute. Even though it is an illegal procedure, there are still some cultures where the girl cannot marry unless she has been circumcised. There may be two procedures involved: clitoridectomy, where part or the entire external clitoris is removed, and infibulation, where the lips of the labia majora are sewn together. The latter will require repeated mutilation, as the husband of the woman will cut her open for her to have sex and to give birth then re-sew her at times when he deems she may be a threat to her purity. Of course, there are the inevitable side effects of infection, and septicaemia may have fatal results. In many parts of the world, infibulation is considered vital and is practised on female infants as the only means that fathers and prospective husbands can ensure that their investment is protected.

Does removal of the clitoris remove a woman's ability to feel sexual arousal? The female clitoris is the only bodily organ with no other known function than providing the woman with pleasure. Maybe this is what is so threatening for men. Similarly, oxytocin, a neuropeptide synthesized by the hypothalamus in the brain and sometimes called the hormone of love, is released during orgasm. This makes a woman feel warm and comfortable and encourages her to keep still after intercourse, giving sperm a greater chance of getting into the Fallopian tubes. Oxytocin is probably the reason that women are more likely to have sex again despite the negative aspects of FGM and childbirth. However, it is worth pointing out that oxytocin flows just as well during a candle-lit dinner for two! This may be one reason for women tending to be less enthusiastic than men about penetrative sex per se.

A study by Lightfoot-Klein (1989) found that FGM was fairly universal in the Sudan, and that it was celebrated with family festivities. It was considered vital to reduce a woman's sex drive, but was also thought to stop her clitoris extending between her legs like a penis. A counsellor may feel shock at the thought of FGM, but it is a normal part of many Islamic and Afro-Caribbean cultures. Before making too many judgements about other cultural practices, we need to remember that in our own culture a hundred years ago women were told on a regular basis by Victorian doctors that sexual desire in women was pathological and could lead to the permanent damage of the sexual organs, the urinary system and the brain. Lightfoot-Klein found from her interviews that even though these women were not allowed to express their pleasure in the sexual act, many did enjoy sex and frequently experienced orgasms. Those who did not said it was due to infection or pain factors in the circumcision site or were unhappy with their marriage.

As discussed in Question 4.5, there are other ways for a woman to have an orgasm than just through clitoral stimulation. So for the client in this question, the counsellor first needs to check out whether the circumcision site has ever been infected or currently gives the client pain. If the answer is yes, she needs to be referred to a gynaecologist. If the answer is no, the assessment questions that are suggested in Question 4.6 may be helpful.

CHAPTER 5

Sexual issues for men

5.1 What sexual problems that men may have can I work with as a therapist, and what sexual problems should I refer elsewhere?

One of the benefits of the unexpected discovery of Viagra, other than the obvious benefit for men hitherto unable to achieve an erection, was that men started to talk more openly about their sexual difficulties. Impotence, as it was previously referred to, used to be hidden with shame and secrecy. Sometimes, men preferred to withdraw from a relationship rather than admit they had a problem making their penis work. A penis working as and when it suits them is one of the male myths that tap into the heart of the macho masculine culture, leaving men who have erectile problems experiencing feelings of inadequacy and worthlessness. It is made worse by the thinking at the time that the majority of men failed to achieve their erections because of psychological factors. It is now known that this is not the case, but the belief contributed to the feelings of inadequacy that men experienced.

When Pfizer were researching a drug called sildenafil to benefit patients with heart disease, they discovered in clinical trials that as a side effect these men were able to achieve erections. The research took a new turn, and, as the tabloid press vaunted a new drug capable of giving men new sexual prowess, the auditors in the NHS became decidedly nervous because they knew how common erectile insufficiency really was. Fearful of how many men would demand access to a new and expensive drug, access to GP prescriptions were limited to only men presenting with a list of physical illnesses that had the effect of making men impotent. That way, they concluded, it would prevent the prohibitive demand from men who only wanted to enhance their sexuality.

I was working in primary care at the time that Viagra (sildenafil) was released onto the market, and what became clear was that rather than men queuing up to see their GP to enhance their sexual prowess, men did present for the first time with genuine and very debilitating sexual difficulties that they had hitherto been unable to discuss. Viagra gave them the permission to be open with their doctors and ask whether it could help them. (The potential of Viagra as a treatment option will be discussed in Question 5.2.)

Men mostly tend to present with sexual issues that fall into two categories:

- problems with sexual desire or arousal that manifest as erectile insufficiency or failure
- problems with ejaculation – too soon, too slow or not at all

As sexual dysfunction may be one of the early indicators of a physical illness, it is preferable that these men are referred to someone with the knowledge and understanding of specialist treatments, which will mean both medical knowledge and psychological understanding and support for a man and his partner. If the counsellor does not have that knowledge and understanding, referral on to a psychosexual therapist is essential. It is not appropriate to spend time exploring this man's upbringing or relationship dynamics without giving him the concomitant medical examinations or access to physical interventions.

* * *

5.2   One of the partners in a gay relationship is still experiencing erectile problems even though he has been prescribed Viagra. What could be going on?

Erectile dysfunction (ED) is one of the most common ailments for men. It is defined as the persistent and recurrent inability to attain or maintain an erection until completion of sexual activity, with marked distress or interpersonal difficulty. In the Massachusetts male-ageing study (Feldman et al., 1994), over 50% of men questioned between the ages of forty and seventy years had experienced ED at some stage in their lives, and 10% were completely impotent. Holmes et al. (1997) estimated the incidence as 5% among men in their forties, 10% of men in their sixties, 20% in their seventies, 30-40% in their eighties and over 50% for men in their nineties. This may not be a manifestation of age per se, but of lifestyle. As erection is a facet of blood flow, poor diet, excessive alcohol, smoking and recreational drugs will all affect a man in his penis in later life. Its incidence exceeds that of coronary heart disease, hypertension and diabetes in the Western world (Hudson-Allez, 1998).

Erection is a complex phenomenon and requires the central nervous system, the vascular system and the hormonal system to be functioning optimally. Disruption in any of these will result in the failure of the penis. The penis is made up of three columns of erectile tissue: two large tubes called the corpora cavernosa and the corpus spongiosum (see Figure 5.1). These tubes maintain the vasocongested blood in the penis to be held at systolic pressure, or slightly above. It requires the relaxation of the smooth muscle, or tunica albuginea, that wraps around the cavernosa within the penis for an erection to occur. As long as this musculature remains relaxed, tumescence is maintained as the muscle walls trap the blood. Hormonally, erection requires testosterone to stimulate and maintain sexual appetite, dehydroepiandrosterone (DHEA) produced by the adrenals to facilitate the production of testosterone, oxytocin and vasopressin excreted by the pituitary gland to potentiate arousal and prostaglandin, which facilitates the erectile vasodilation. Men may lose their erection, or may be unable to achieve an erection, when the vascular reflex system fails to pump blood into the corpora cavernosa. Alternatively, the blood may flow in the penis and out again too quickly in a venous leak, thus preventing the penis from becoming or staying erect.

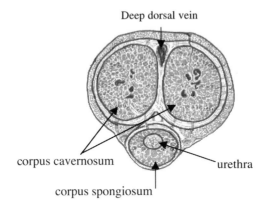

Deep dorsal vein

corpus cavernosum

urethra

corpus spongiosum

Figure 5.1 Cross-section of a penis.

There are three forms of erectile difficulties – psychogenic, resulting from psychological difficulties, organic, resulting from physical problems, and a combination of the two. It is thought that up to 90% of all erectile problems are organic, with the remainder being purely psychogenic (Brindley, 1996; Costa et al., 1997), although up to 25% of erectile failure is considered iatrogenic, caused by medication like antidepressants, steroids and barbiturates (O'Keefe and Hunt, 1985). We also know that 50% of diabetics experience erectile failure, so blood sugar needs to be checked in all cases. Other physical causes are electro-convulsive therapy, Addison's disease, coronary heart disease, hypothyroidism, multiple sclerosis, Parkinson's disease, depression and emphysema. Indeed, it is a shame that GPs fail to ask routinely about a man's ability to achieve his erection, as it may be one of the first indicators that something more sinister may be going on in the man's physical well-being.

Compassionate questioning will determine whether the erectile difficulty has been a lifelong (primary) problem or whether it is the result of change (secondary), and whether it occurs generally or only in specific situations. If questioning determines that it had a sudden onset under specific situations, yet nocturnal or early-morning erections are unaffected, the problem is likely to be psychogenic. If, however, the problem had a slow onset, was consistently present without nocturnal or early-morning erections, yet libido appears to be unaffected, the problem is likely to be organic.

Useful questions for a counsellor to ask him for assessment of his situation would be:

- Does he wake at night or in the morning with an erection?
- Has he ever had an erection?
- Can he get an erection under any circumstances? If so, is the erection full or partial?
- Is the erect penis straight? (see Question 5.6)
- Can he get an erection while masturbating or fantasizing?
- Does he get an erection on his own and lose it at a particular time?
- Has he had a medical check-up for diabetes?

If he has always suffered with erectile problems, that is, if it is primary, it may be useful to ask:

- Is he comfortable with his sexual orientation?
- Does he experience a tight foreskin or pain on ejaculation?
- Does he fear penetration?
- Has there been any past sexual trauma?

If the ED is secondary, it may be useful to ask:

- Has he experienced any losses?
- Is he depressed?
- Is he feeling anxious or obsessional?
- Is he taking any prescribed medication?
- Has he had any recent illnesses or operations (cutting through vital abdominal nerve endings)?
- Has he experienced premature ejaculation (which often precedes

erectile failure as the man gets into a pattern of performance anxiety, or 'willie-watching')?
- Has he adolescent children (competition and rivalry)?

What treatments are there available for ED? All organic causes of ED need referral to a urologist, who may suggest one of the following:

- *Oral therapy*, e.g. Viagra, Cialis, Uprima, Levitra, Yohimbine. Although not readily available on the NHS for men with psychogenic ED, they can be obtained on private prescription and via the Internet. These are effective in up to 86% of cases.
- *Intracavernosal injections* of prostaglandin, e.g. Caverject. Still popular with many men, despite Viagra, which is contraindicated for men with heart disease. Some men prefer the local injection as opposed to a pill, which goes through the whole body system. Men having penile injections need to be warned of the danger of a priapism, which is prolonged and painful erection that does not detumesce. More than four hours would require a visit to a hospital A & E centre for blood reduction. Repeated injections to the same site on the penis may also cause plaque to build up and a subsequent curvature of the penis.
- *Transurethral therapy*, i.e. MUSE (Medicated Urethral System for Erection). The same drug as Caverject, without the skin trauma, MUSE is a pellet that is popped down the end of the penis into the urethra and then melts into the corpora. Not as effective as intracavernosal injections (50%) and has the hindrance of requiring the man to walk around for fifteen or so minutes to encourage the blood flow, which plays havoc with foreplay.
- A *nasal spray*, currently being developed by the pharmaceutical industry, is now developing supposedly suitable for both men and women (PT-141). Watch this space!
- *Vacuum pumps* are devices that fit over the penis and pull blood into it as a result of a vacuum in the tube. A tight rubber ring is then placed over the penis to prevent the blood flowing back out again. These devices are considered safe, but the penis has an unnatural swing to it, as the erection terminates at the rubber band rather than at the base of the penile shaft. In addition, men may experience their penis as cold, as there is no natural blood circulation.
- *Prostheses* are very much the last resort of erectile treatments because, if they fail, there is no return to other treatments afterwards, owing to the permanent damage done to the corpora. There are two types of prosthetic: a cheaper version (usually, but not always, NHS), which comprises two malleable rods giving the man a permanent erection. This may not be suitable for those men who like to swim a lot or spend time with children, in case it is misunderstood. Alternatively, the more upmarket version consists of a pump placed within the scrotum, which

allows the man to pump himself up and later push it back down again. The body rejecting artificial aids is always an issue in these cases.

The medicalization of all these different forms of treatment for ED has meant that there is a tendency for urologists to respond as if the problem is solved once the erection has returned. This takes a reductionist approach to the issue and ignores the ability of the man to translate his newly achieved erection into successful sexual activity.

In this question, one partner in a gay relationship has been prescribed Viagra (sildenafil) but is still not achieving an erection. In order for Viagra to be effective, the man still has to feel sexual desire. Viagra works by relaxing the smooth muscle; so it helps with the mechanics but not with the other arousal dimensions. It helps in therapy if men understand that it is a myth to think that a man can have an erection at any time, in any place, with any partner. It is also a myth to think that all erectile problems are in the penis. They are sometimes due to the person's struggling with their own sexuality, with deep emotional feelings, like shame or rage, or it may be that the partner is no longer attractive to him.

Similarly, the problem may be in the partner himself. Sometimes partners react in a very negative way to an artificially achieved erection. The reason for this is that, when he (or she) views the partner's erection, this is an indication to the partner that he (or she) is desirable. If the man has therefore obtained this erection in the privacy of the bathroom, that aspect of desirability is omitted from the couple dynamic. A response may therefore be, 'If you can do that on your own, you can do the rest on your own as well!'

Finally, there may be an issue in the relationship itself. Is this gay relationship a monogamous one? Are there sexual health fears or power struggles going on? Thus, helping a man achieve a suitable erection is not just a medical phenomenon, but needs the help and support of a therapist, whether a counsellor or psychosexual therapist, to translate the medical intervention into something that they can do together and to investigate the inevitable subconscious dynamics within the partnership.

* * *

5.3   I am seeing a young man who ejaculates as soon as he enters his wife's vagina. Is this a physical or a psychological problem? And, if the latter, can I as a non-specialist therapist be of any help?

Premature ejaculation (PE) is ejaculation that occurs sooner than the couple would wish, either before vaginal penetration, at the point of penetration or within the first few thrusts of penetration. One-third of adult males report that they ejaculate earlier than they would like, and it is a problem in both heterosexual and homosexual couples. The cause of PE is usually psychogenic, with a combination of performance anxiety, shame of performance anxiety (Apfelbaum, 1983), a history of rapid masturbation or feelings of anxiety and guilt leading to a conditioned loss of control. There are physical causes, however. Multiple sclerosis, diabetes, Parkinson's disease, spina bifida and hormonal deficiencies can all produce this symptom.

Useful assessment questions for a counsellor to ask a client presenting with PE would be:

• When does ejaculation occur?
• After how many thrusts does he ejaculate?
• Does or did he masturbate rapidly?
• Was guilt associated with masturbation?
• Does anything help ejaculation, like alcohol or thoughts?
• Does anything make the problem worse, like tiredness or alcohol?
• Is it pleasurable?
• Is the foreskin tight when the penis is erect?
• Is there pain or fear of penetration?

The prescription of some SSRIs (Specific Serotonin Reuptake Inhibitors), like fluoxetine or paroxetine, has been used as an adjunct to psychosexual therapy because one of the side effects of SSRIs is to retard ejaculation. However, the drug is not taken on a daily basis as if being taken for depression but taken a couple of hours before sexual intercourse. There is also a product called Prolong: stretchable plastic penile rings with a ribbed plate that fit over the penis. It is designed to attenuate the over-sensitivity of the penis through the process of habituation. There are few clinical trials that demonstrate its efficacy at present, however.

A counsellor can offer a lot of supportive help for a man presenting with PE. The assessment questions will help determine whether the cause is likely to be psychogenic or organic. The latter case will need a referral to the GP for urological interventions. However, for those men who do suffer with anxiety, guilt or fear, some insight into the reasons for this will be immensely helpful, as will be learning relaxation exercises. Once calmer, he needs to learn to recognize the point of inevitability to develop ejaculatory control. This is the point between the two phases of ejaculation: the first is the emission phase when the semen collects at the base of the prostate bulb; the second is the ejaculatory phase as the muscular contractions pump the semen out. The second phase is beyond voluntary control, so in order for a man to develop ejaculatory control, he needs to become aware of the emission phase. Cognitive behavioural work that teaches him to practise stopping when he reaches the emission phase is a treatment option, although a counsellor can offer some useful support by encouraging the man to relax during intercourse, distracting his thoughts from worrying about what his penis is doing and focusing on his successes rather than his perceived failures.

* * *

5.4   A male client of mine in his twenties can have an erection when making love but cannot ejaculate. Is this likely to be a psychological or a physical problem?

It sounds as if this young man is experiencing retarded ejaculation (RE). This occurs when a man can have a firm, sustained erection but is unable to ejaculate and has occasionally been called quasi-priapism. These sustained erections are present even if he feels repelled by, or angry with, his partner, which is a very common psychological cause of this phenomenon. There may be, however, iatrogenic causes from medication, although there can be organic causes from lesions in the genito-urinary tract or spinal chord, or damage to the lumbar system. The incidence of RE is low, and thought to be just 1–2% of clinical populations.

Useful questions for the counsellor to ask at assessment may be:

- Has he ever been able to ejaculate?
- Can he ejaculate under any circumstances?
- Is he taking prescribed medication?
- If masturbation produces ejaculation, does it require such severity that vaginal thrusting will not work?
- If he does not ejaculate, does he experience orgasm? (If yes, see Question 5.5)
- Is ejaculation pleasurable?

Introducing these questions initially will aid the client in formulating the presentation to the specialist and will also allow the counsellor to be clearer about to whom to refer.

Cognitive Behaviour Therapy or psychodynamic therapy with a psychosexual therapist should be considered for psychogenic RE to ascertain why he is 'withholding' and whether underlying anger, either with his partner or with women in general, is an issue. It may also be due to performance pressure, ambivalence in the relationship, power struggles or demands for conception. For potential organic causes, refer to urologists, who have used more aggressive techniques like electrical stimulation of the prostate with an anal probe, but with varying success.

* * *

5.5   One of my male clients is distressed because during sex he reaches a climax but no ejaculate is expelled. What might be the cause of this?

It could be that this client is experiencing retrograde ejaculation, sometimes called injaculation. This is when the sphincter at the base of the bladder fails to close during orgasm and the expelled semen flows into the bladder instead of out through the urethra. This can be due to iatrogenic causes, like prostate surgery or medication. It is thought that the incidence of retrograde ejaculation after transurethral prostatectomy is 80% (Eardley, 2004). Or it may be due to physical causes like bladder neck incompetence, spinal cord lesions, diabetes or multiple sclerosis.

However, the ability for men to have an orgasm has taken on a new twist with the fashionable concept of Tantric sex. First the man discourages the expulsion of his ejaculate by holding his pubococcygeal muscle, so he only experiences the orgasm. Thus he learns by will to force the semen into the bladder. Tantric sex was developed from Hindu culture and involves the revering of the female goddess Shakti. It has developed into a feminizing of sexual behaviour, thus, the ability to have orgasm without ejaculation. A Tantric sex master would not have sex with a woman unless she was fully sexually aroused, and the prohibition of ejaculation means that the man can continue to have sex until he is sure that she is fully sexually satiated. However, some Tantric sex practitioners have taken it too far and brag about being able to continue with sexual activity for hours without respite. Whereas some women complain that men who stop intercourse when they ejaculate may not have gone on for long enough for them to achieve an orgasm, there will be few women who will want to continue with intercourse for hours on end, without getting sore and bored. Again, these men have overemphasized the importance of penetrative sex, which may not be shared by their female partner.

The client in this case expresses his distress because he is not expelling his ejaculate. If he is a young man, and may wish later to father children, then it becomes a serious issue and needs to be referred back to his GP for a urological referral. If he has no wish to father children, then a frank discussion of the physiology may allay some of his distress. If the problem is due to his medication, then changing to a different agent may help. Alternatively, he may look on the positive side that he is achieving without effort what the Tantric master takes years to perfect!

* * *

5.6   A female client I have been seeing experiences pain during penetrative sex, and so her husband sent her for treatment. But it seems to me from what she has said that his penis has a curve in it. Which one has the problem?

A man's penis should be straight when it is erect for successful vaginal penetration. If the penis has a curve in it, during sexual penetration it hits on the side of the vaginal wall causing pain and discomfort to the both of them. Peyronie's disease is the presence of dense fibrous plaques within the shaft of the penis, causing it to be lumpy and to bend, which in some cases may cause the man pain when he achieves an erection. Eventually, he will lose his ability to have an erection, as the plaque will interfere with the cavernous tissue. The condition is most common in men between the ages of 40 and 69. The incidence in men is unknown because many men fail to attend for help because of embarrassment. Additionally, a man's penis needs to be erect for a GP to diagnose it. The cause of Peyronie's disease is unclear, but it has been linked to an autoimmune disorder, a hereditary link and the normal ageing process (Ahmed, 1997), although there is a known iatrogenic cause following repeated trauma to the penis as a result of intracavernosal injections. For some men the disease is self-limiting, whereas in others it can be progressive. Pharmacological, ultrasound and radiological treatments have been tried with mixed success, as has the repeated use of vacuum therapy, but the most common intervention is corrective surgery for men who cannot have sexual intercourse as a result of excessive penile curvature. However, surgery has the complication of shortening the penis, which for some men can be unacceptable.

As the client in this case is the wife of a man who may have Peyronie's disease, it may be that the counsellor will need to encourage the client to respectively encourage her husband to seek a medical diagnosis. The client may ask her husband to attend counselling as a couple so that a full discussion regarding their sexual difficulties can take place. Encouraging neither to see it as each other's problem, but a shared difficulty in the sexual repertoire, can reduce guilt and blame in the couple dynamic.

* * *

5.7   A male client I see is having surgery for an enlarged prostate. He is fearful that he will be impotent after the operation. Are his fears justified?

The prostate gland is a fibromuscular bulbous structure situated at the base of the penis (see Figure 5.2), beneath the bladder. The prostate contributes fluid to the seminal ejaculate. Stimulation of the prostate enhances male sexual arousal and is used by many men as a male G-spot (Margolis, 2004).

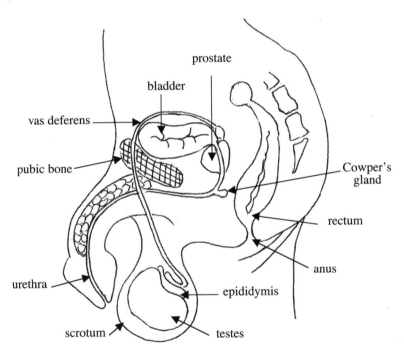

Figure 5.2 The male pelvic organs.

Problems with the prostate are usually detected by a digital rectal examination, which may account for many men's reluctance to have routine checks on their prostate. However, determining the man's PSA (prostate-specific antigen) levels through blood tests may encourage men to attend for regular screening. The PSA is a protein produced by the cells of the prostate. When it enlarges, the PSA levels rise. However, research has shown that it is not the PSA level per se that can determine cancer, as it may increase and fall again leading to false positive tests. It is the PSA level velocity, or change over time that is important for the detection of malignancy (Eastham et al., 2003).

Problems with the prostate account for up to a quarter of all visits to urologists (Kirby, 1996) and are grouped into three categories: benign prostatic hyperplasia, prostate cancer and prostatitis syndromes, which are usually, but not always, bacterial infections or inflammation. When the prostate enlarges, it compresses and obstructs the urethra, impeding the flow of urine. This in turn can weaken the bladder and backpressure can affect the kidneys and cause infection. The most common form of treatment for the more serious conditions is a prostatectomy. There are four types of surgery:

- transurethral prostatectomy: usually using lasers through the urethral tube
- suprapubic prostatectomy: incision in the abdomen through the bladder
- retropubic prostatectomy: abdominal incision to gain access to the prostate in between pubic bone and bladder
- perineal prostatectomy: incision through the perineum (usually for radical clearance of malignant tissue)

Abdominal incisions tend to cut through essential nerve endings, resulting in erectile difficulties, and it used to be considered that any man having a prostatectomy would be rendered impotent. Similarly, the radical procedure via the perineum damages the neuronal pathways and impotence is inevitable. However, the more modern transurethral procedures have reduced the incidence of erectile problems drastically, although there is a high chance of developing retrograde ejaculation (Eardley, 2004). If the original problem was cancer, treatment may also involve anti-androgens, as androgens feed prostatic cancer. However, the effect of anti-androgen treatment is likely to be a loss of libido.

The client in this case is worried that his surgery will affect his ability to achieve an erection post-operatively. It would be helpful if the counsellor can encourage the client to express those fears to the surgeon in advance of the surgery, as this may well influence the type of procedure that is undertaken. A frank discussion with his health practitioner may help allay some of his fears. If he has a partner, it may also help to involve the partner in discussions for further reassurance.

* * *

5.8   I am seeing a 55-year-old man whose partner is fifteen years younger than him and he is afraid that if he doesn't have sex with her three times a week she will reject him for a younger man. Is it not usual for a man to have less sex as he gets older? What's his problem?

The client in this question is 55 years of age and his partner is 40. A woman in her forties has reached her sexual peak; so she may be enjoying her thrice-weekly sexual activity. It is not known whether this is a new relationship. If it is, they may still be in the lustful stage of their relationship. Also, it is not known how frequently he used to have sex. Some adolescents and young men want to make love every day, therefore his sexual frequency may have reduced as he has got older. Alternatively, he may be putting himself under unnecessary pressure to perform for fear of losing her. There is no problem here if both partners are happy with what is happening between them.

* * *

5.9   I am seeing a couple where the husband is a diabetic and is about to have a penile prosthesis. What issues are this couple likely to encounter?

Prostheses are generally considered to be the last resort of all interventions for erectile failure. If the surgery is conducted on the NHS, it is likely the urologist will use the cheaper malleable penile prosthesis. This consists of two flexible rods inserted into the penile shaft to give a permanent erection but can be adjusted in various positions. These are not suitable for the well-endowed but are able to be trimmed to fit the smaller individual's size. Malleable prostheses are effective, safe and have a very low failure rate (Witherow, 1996).

However, privately funded surgery will more likely opt for the more expensive inflatable penile prostheses, which are in three parts, with a pump, a saline reservoir and the penile shaft. The pump, placed in the scrotum, allows the patient to pump the erection as and when appropriate, and reverse it when love-making has ended. However, the more complex technology is, the greater the risk of mechanical failure or fluid leakage with the inflatable prosthesis. Yet it has a much lower erosion rate than the malleable device. Furthermore, some urologists are against the cheaper variety, arguing that it is not appropriate for a man who may want to swim, sunbathe or mix with children, when a permanent erection can be misconstrued. The worst problem with prostheses is that it is the last-resort intervention for erectile failure, and they are not always successful. If they have to be removed, the chances of having a subsequent erection are minimal, as the corpora will have been irreparably damaged, although some clinicians have found that a vacuum pump may have limited success thereafter (Nadig, 1986).

The counsellor in this case can help the client discuss which form of prosthesis the client would like and assist the couple in coming to terms with what might feel like an alien appendage. Encouraging the partner to help the man to achieve an erection by pumping the scrotum at the appropriate time will allow the partner to feel that she, or he, is participating in the arousal dynamic and contributing to the foreplay prior to making love.

CHAPTER 6

Sex and relationships

6.1 When I am seeing a couple who are experiencing difficulties, I imagine their sexual relationship might well be an important factor. If they don't talk about it with me, what might it be useful for me to know?

When a couple first fall in love with each other, the warmth and intensity of their limerance, demonstrated by preoccupied thoughts, acute longing, feelings of walking on air and focusing on positive attributes (Tennot, 1979) allows them to overlook any idiosyncrasy that the partner may have. Objectivity in relating to each other's personality traits becomes subsumed with the desire of wanting to be together and connect with each other, both sexually and emotionally. As the intensity of the lust starts to wane, however, objectivity starts to return and appraisal of the partner's views, behaviour and lifestyle start to be formulated. Dissimilarities in culture, upbringing, politics etc., which might originally have been thought to be endearing, now may prove an irritant. Most personality traits have a downside, for example a person drawn to a partner who is solid, safe and reliable may later also experience this person as rigid or boring. A person who is dynamic, gregarious, flirtatious and fun may later prove to have an issue with commitment or may be disloyal or unfaithful. These difficulties may manifest themselves in either a reduction in intimate and sexual behaviour creating a feeling of emotional estrangement, or one of the partners may develop a specific sexual dysfunction that will interrupt or inhibit sexual activity.

As one works through the difficulties that the couple face, it may be useful for the counsellor to make an assessment of each partner's attachment style. Half a century ago, Bowlby (1951) first discussed the process of monotropy (or imprinting) in an infant's attachment to his or her mother, which was later operationalized in the famous Ainsworth (1979) Strange Situation Studies.

Bowlby's (and later Winnicott's 1960) theory of how an infant attached to the mother at a critical stage of development has now been provided with physiological evidence from MRI scanning of the brain from neuropsychological research (Schore, 1994). These data underpin the theories of attachment style; how an infant attaches with the mother is mirrored by the later attachment style within relationships when the child reaches adulthood (Fonaghy, 2001). Ainsworth's studies suggested that 70% of infants in her studies were securely attached, leaving nearly a third of individuals insecurely attached and thus having the potential to experience difficulties within their adult relationships. It is now thought that for insecurely attached individuals their mothers need not have been physically absent per se but may have been physically or emotionally unavailable to the child, for example because of work or post-natal depression, during the critical practising period of autonomy, thought to be between twelve and eighteen months (Shore, 1994). The feelings of abandonment and rejection that are built up in an insecurely attached child manifest themselves in adult relationships, especially during sexual activity, a time when a person becomes the most exposed and the most vulnerable. Knowing whether a member of the couple is avoidantly, ambivalently or fearfully attached to the partner will help the counsellor and the couple identify the dynamics of the relationship and may also help to determine whether they are acting out issues from their family of origin.

Seeing a couple who are experiencing difficulties in the relationship can be challenging for the counsellor and requires specific skills training. A counsellor who sees gay and lesbian as well as heterosexual couples also requires a clear understanding of the differences in the dynamics and strains that these couples face. Crowe and Ridley (1990) have written an excellent overview of working with couples using a behavioural-systems approach, Beck (1988) from a cognitive perspective, and Daines and Perrett (2000) offer strategies from a psychodynamic perspective.

* * *

6.2   I am seeing a couple who are expecting their first child. They are very close but recently admitted that they have stopped having sex because he was losing his erections. However, he is less worried about it than she is. What is going on?

In Question 3.4, I discussed the difficulties that having a child may bring to a relationship, and Question 5.2 discusses the problems of erectile dysfunction (ED). What is interesting in this presenting couple is the dynamic occurring between them. Usually, if a man is experiencing erectile failure, he feels unhappy about himself, has a sense of inadequacy and a loss of masculinity. But, with this couple, the man does not seem to be too concerned. This demonstrates how essential it is for the counsellor to look beyond the presenting problem and not simply go down the track of enabling this man to get his penis to work with pharmacological or external interventions. It may be more valuable for the counsellor to consider what purpose this sexual dysfunction serves. Has he developed this problem for a reason? Currently, penetrative sex cannot take place, but the couple remain very close, and it is not affecting their relationship. Presumably, she has initiated the counselling because she is more concerned about 'his problem' than he is.

It may therefore be useful for the counsellor to explore what he is protecting his wife from by not being able to penetrate her. Perhaps he fears he will harm the child with penetrative sex and may therefore need some information. Perhaps he fears he will hurt his wife during intercourse, in which case the counsellor could provide specific suggestions on sexual positions they may find more comfortable. Or maybe there is some deeper issue that needs to be addressed, as the woman moves from the role of lover to mother, that is manifest in a somatic way. Or perhaps he does not have an issue at all, but she has, and his body is protecting her from herself. It is therefore valuable for the counsellor to make a full and thorough clinical assessment and sexual history of both partners before embarking on a course of interventions.

* * *

6.3 A common problem I find in counselling couples is that one of the pair wants sex more often than the other and this causes tension between them. How do I know when someone wants sex too much?

There are two issues within this question that need to be teased out. First, how much sex is too much and how do we know that the amount of sex a person requires is too much? Second, even if neither partner has a pathological problem with their sexual requirements, how do we help a couple whose sexual requirements are not compatible?

The problem of wanting or needing too much sex is called a plethora of names in the literature: a hypersexual state, nymphomania, Casanova syndrome, Don Juan syndrome, satyriasis, hypererotocism, hyperlibido, sexual compulsivity, sexual impulsive disorder and many more such terms. But how much sex is too much? Some researchers have tried to quantify it, like Moore and May (1982), who counted how many orgasms a man has each week. They determined 0.2% of their sample had more than 21. Although three a day may be on the high side for a middle-aged married man, it is unlikely to be considered excessive for an unattached young man, irrespective of sexuality, with ample opportunity for performance. Similarly, Kafka (1997) operationalized hypersexuality for men to seven or more sexual experiences per week for a minimum of six months after the age of fifteen years. This does seem to be on the low side for a young man, although Kafka also pointed out that the hypersexualized behaviour must be long term, distressing, dysfunctional and independent of any other psychiatric condition or substance misuse.

What makes hypersexuality pathological is not how often the person has sex but whether the sexual behaviour leads to distress or disruption to normal living. Barth and Kinder (1987) agree that excessive sexual behaviour will be disrupting of the individual's life in such a way that the individual derives no lasting satisfaction from the sexual act. The controversies in the literature that underpin the nosology of the problem seem to focus around whether it is an expression of low or high levels of desire, whether levels of satisfaction are not being met or whether it is addictive or compulsive behaviour. Rinehart and McCabe (1997) found in a survey that those engaging in high-frequency masturbation or sexual intercourse were less satisfied than their low-frequency counterparts, suggesting that hypersexuality is associated with insatiability. They found no correlation, however, between high frequency and anxiety or fear of intimacy, but they did find a relationship between deviant sexuality and depression.

Are there physical causes to hypersexuality? It has been observed in patients with neurological damage, organic brain disease, infectious diseases and manic and psychotic states. It also has iatrogenic causes, for example medical interventions for rabies, tuberculosis and syphilis have been associated with high sexual activity. Recent research conducted at the Kinsey Institute by Bancroft and Vukadinovic (2004) has focused on the relationship between mood and sexuality and found it was more variable than previously held. Whereas the majority of men report a decrease in sexual interest when depressed or anxious, 15-25% report an increase. Nearly a quarter is quite a considerable figure, and these men may be more likely to pursue sexual interaction when in a negative mood state. These findings may add a physiological underpinning to the complexity of 'out of control' and high-risk sexual behaviour (see Question 6.5).

Therefore, it would be helpful if the counsellor tries to determine whether the sexual behaviour is hypersexual by the demand requirements of the one partner in comparison with the other. If it is considered that the demands are higher than the usual range for an individual, the work can progress as outlined in the answer to Question 9.2. If, however, the demands do not appear excessive, yet are more than the other partner would wish, the counsellor is dealing with a not uncommon phenomenon.

In the answer to Question 2.4 the various ranges of sexual arousal were discussed, as well as how women's and men's arousal levels skew at opposite ends of a normal arousal range. This inevitably means that it is a 'normal' and common phenomenon for there to be a discrepancy between how often each partner in a heterosexual couple may want to make love. The scenario presented by such a couple becomes familiar: he asks for sex more often because he is expressing his love through sex. For her, caring and sharing are more important than sex, and so she does not want to be sexual all the time. She can show her love in other ways. The more he urges or presses for sex, the more pressured she feels, and so she starts to withdraw from other intimate acts. Hugs and kisses are avoided in case they are taken as a prelude to sex. The more she withdraws, the more rejected he feels. He rationalizes that he has to keep asking for sex more often because he never knows when he is going to get it next. The pressure is increased between them and so is the withdrawal. Sex stops happening altogether, and the rift between them becomes an unmentionable chasm.

The therapeutic intervention, developed by Crowe and Ridley (1986), most suited for this difficulty is deceptively simple but extremely effective. The counsellor asks each partner how often he or she would like to make love. Suppose he says four times a week and she says once a week, a compromise between the two is made, say twice a week. Sexual dates are then timetabled into the week to make allowances for work pressures and children's activities. Increasingly, my own finding is that double-income families are not sexual during the week, as they are too exhausted to bother, owing to work pressures, children and domestic demands. Thus they are more likely to choose the weekend for these two dates. Assume that they choose Friday night and Sunday morning as their time to be intimate or sexual. The ground rules are that she must be sexual on those planned times. This also gives her the time she needs to cognitively think herself into sexual arousal. On the other days, he must not ask for sex even if she gets close to him. This allows for the closeness and intimacy to return because she knows he is not going to ask for sex. The pressure is taken away and she becomes more willing to kiss and cuddle. He stops needing to ask for sex because he does know when he is going to get it next, and he no longer feels rejected. The couple can become close again. Of course, when first introduced to this idea, one of the couple may object, saying he or she wants or prefers spontaneous rather than planned sex. But if they are asked what they would prefer to do, given they are having no sex, they tend reluctantly to give it a try and are invariably pleased with the result. Of course, the timetabling for sex does not have to last for long, but it gets the two partners back into the routine of being sexual again on a regular basis, and they tend to be more careful about making time for each other in the future.

* * *

6.4   A woman I am seeing who is in a lesbian relationship has flashbacks of childhood sexual abuse when she is having sex with her partner. Yet her abuser was her father. Is this usual?

Many studies have been conducted over the years to try to determine whether early childhood sexual abuse leads to homosexuality in adulthood, and the results are always ambiguous. For example, Gundlach (1977) found in a survey of 450 women that of those who were sexually abused by a male relative, 94% had lesbian orientation. Yet Herman (1981) conducted a study of father-daughter incest victims and found only 5% were lesbian. There are some who suggest that being abused as children predisposes women to homosexuality because they grow up with phobic reactions to sexual activity, with a strong hatred of men (Jehu, 1988). The lesbian community, however, are likely to be less than happy with these interpretations as they pathologize their behaviour and suggest that their sexual orientation can be 'cured'. A homosexual orientation is not developed simply as a result of aversive experiences; it is far more complex than that.

Lesbian women who have been sexually abused in childhood will respond predominantly in the same way as heterosexual women. Flashbacks that may occur during sexual activity with a chosen partner as the result of traumatization are common, especially if the abuse occurred before the child was aged three where the memories are laid out sensorially in the right hemisphere of the brain that has no verbal access (Schore, 1994). These memories may be triggered by bodily touches, smells, sounds etc. rather than by the visual appearance of the partner. Hall (1999) also describes such women dissociating during sexual activity, which has repercussions on sexual arousal and sexual satisfaction. By the counsellor working through the trauma in a sensitive and supportive way, as discussed by Bass and Davies (1988), this will help this woman deal with her abuse issues. Her sexuality should not be considered an issue unless she has a problem with it.

* * *

6.5 A gay couple I am seeing are very volatile in their relationship and punish each other by sleeping with other men. They both are very fearful that this behaviour will lead to the destruction of their relationship but cannot seem to stop themselves. Is this intensity a feature of being gay?

In the answer to Question 6.1, I suggested that it is important to have an understanding of couple relationships; this includes an understanding of the dynamic of homosexual couples as being essential for a counsellor who wishes to work with gay men. It is inappropriate to use the anti-discriminatory premise of treating them the same as heterosexual couples. It could be considered discriminatory to regard gay men's needs as unnatural, or less important, but is equally discriminatory to suggest that they are the same as a heterosexual couple and not to acknowledge that they have different issues to work through as a couple. McWhirter and Mattison (1984) provide a valuable insight into gay couples who are not in the process of therapy, and identify a very clear developmental progression through their relationships. From this and other studies, they found that expectations of sexual exclusivity are not necessarily assumed in such relationships. They are less likely to follow the monogamous way of relating; sex is less important than the protection of intimacy, and there is an understanding that sexual needs can be met from outside the relationship. Gay relationships are crucially based on choice and equality; so it is essential for the counsellor to determine whether any spoken or unspoken ground rules have been formulated in the early stages of the relationship and whether these have changed in any way.

Recent research from the Kinsey Institute (Bancroft et al., 2003a) has shown that around 10–20% of men, irrespective of their sexuality, have neuronal responses that lead to sexual arousal during times when they feel stress, guilt, anxiety or depression. This comes from research that has investigated why some men, most commonly gay men, take risks with unprotected sex despite all the warnings regarding HIV and AIDS. Farley (1986) categorizes these men as 'type T', or thrill-seeking/risk-taking personalities. He argues that these men do not want 'safe' sex, as safety takes the thrill out of the behaviour.

We know that a loss of libido is a common symptom in the majority of people during emotional times. However, with the particular men in this study, their antithetical behaviour may have made them wish to engage in more sexual behaviour than before. This will then have a cyclical effect, as the more sexually active they become, the more risk-taking is incurred both for the individual's own health and for the relationship; the more stress and anxiety is provoked, the more this leads to even more sexual behaviour (see Figure 6.1). This finding clearly has important implications in terms of helping couples deal with relationship-destructive behaviour and also goes a long way in explaining why individuals indulge in personal risk in the anonymous, unprotected sex scene prevalent within the gay community, and also offers an explanation of why some men get addicted to Internet pornography (see Question 9.2).

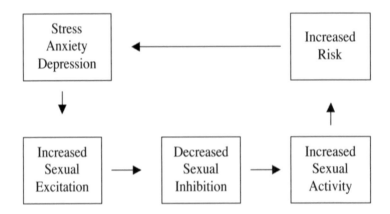

Figure 6.1 Cycle of increased sexual activity, after Bancroft et al. (2003a).

Of course, it is wise not to assume that any man who does not want to use a condom must be a type T personality. There are many reasons why men prefer not to use condoms. They may feel that condoms inhibit the spontaneity of love-making or may reduce the sensitivity and experience of friction. Some have a belief system that values the sharing of bodily fluids and emissions as a process of the union. And still others may find that the smell or touch of a condom is unpleasant; indeed, they may even be allergic to the latex. There are microbicides currently being developed that kill the viruses which lead to infections that may eventually take the place of the condom. These are placed in a lubricant like KY jelly and make a physical barrier between the infection and the body. Although they are unlikely to be as effective as condoms in practice, there is still the potential to produce huge reductions in HIV transmission for those who will not use condoms. However, the current emphasis is on the development of vaginal microbicides rather than rectal ones, as it is argued that to do so would be to condone sex without the use of condoms (Forbes, 2004).

If the counsellor feels that the client is a person who becomes aroused by stress, or is a frequent risk-taker, some useful work that may be undertaken with the couple is in helping to divert this tendency into other forms of risk-taking, like high-thrill/risk sports, which could then protect the person's sexual health and relationship. Working on the tensions within the relationship may also help reduce the stress and tension and therefore reduce the volatility and the desire to be sexual outside of the relationship.

* * *

6.6 I am seeing a couple who are on the brink of splitting up because the wife, who is 41, has become pregnant. She is delighted and sees it as her last chance for motherhood. Her husband, however, is furious because he had a vasectomy five years ago and insists she must have been having an affair. He has no wish for another child, let alone, as he puts it, 'someone else's bastard'. How can I help this couple resolve their fundamental differences when this situation can offer no compromise?

This is a difficult situation for a couple who are experiencing a crisis event that could destroy their relationship. First, it would help them if the counsellor were to offer some information to the couple regarding the ability to spontaneously conceive following vasectomy. A vasectomy is a minor surgical procedure that cuts the vas deferens, the tubes that deliver the sperm from the testes in a man, and is a common method of choice for a couple for permanent contraception. During the surgery, the clipped ends of the vas deferens are tied, clipped or cauterized with a laser. There have been numerous documented cases, however, where a man's vas deferens has re-healed and conception has occurred as a consequence. Although rare (there is a 0.2% failure rate), it can happen. This man could have his semen tested following the confirmation of pregnancy, and, should his sperm count still be found to be extremely low, this may indeed question his wife's protestations of innocence. Otherwise, a DNA test would be able to determine the child's parentage without any doubt.

However, there is another issue that is dividing this couple. Even if it could be proved that the baby was the husband's child, he may still say he does not want it. Presumably he is of a similar age to his wife, and he may have been looking forward to the time when their other children were growing up and leaving home: a time when the couple can reunite as a unit and spend time doing things together without the distraction of children. He therefore may view the thought of another pregnancy with trepidation, not wishing to start all over again becoming the father of a teenager as he approaches his sixties.

His wife, on the other hand, has a biological clock that is running down. Unlike her husband, her fertility is about to reduce drastically as she approaches her peri-menopausal decade. Women of this age often ruminate as to whether to have a last child before that decision is taken away from them. She may also feel less valuable as a parent at a time when her other children have developed into autonomous individuals and are making their own way in the world; this is commonly called 'empty-nest syndrome'. She may therefore be thrilled at this unexpected event, which has taken away the necessity of having to make a difficult decision, and she may find the thought of a termination abhorrent.

This is a difficult situation for the counsellor because there is no compromise between having a child and not having one. However, taking the heat out of the situation by determining the parentage of the child may help the couple discuss the situation more rationally, and perhaps reach a conclusion that does not end in splitting the relationship apart.

* * *

6.7   I find that a lot of women I see who are on the contraceptive pill are less interested in sex, which has an inevitable effect on their relationship. Yet, when I discuss with the couple alternative methods of contraception, they both seem unwilling to change for fear of unwanted pregnancies. Are other methods of contraception as effective as the pill?

There are now many methods of preventing unwanted pregnancies, which can be grouped into hormonal methods, inter-uterine devices, barrier devices, behavioural methods and permanent surgical procedures.

The pill is a very successful contraceptive method, with a failure rate of just 1%, providing it is taken consistently and correctly. There are two types of pill: a combination of oestrogen and progesterone, and progesterone-only pills. The combination pill works by preventing ovulation and thickening the cervical mucus to inhibit the sperm, whereas the progesterone-only pill does not inhibit ovulation. All hormonal methods of contraception have the potential to change appetite and therefore affect weight, with a secondary effect of changing sexual desire. Some women also experience fluid retention and breast tenderness, and the pill may also aggravate depression. Another hormonal method is an injection of depot-medroxyprogesterone acetate (DMPA), often called a 'depot injection' after the trade name of Depo-Provera. This injection lasts twelve weeks and is one of the most effective methods of birth control, with a minimal failure rate of 0.3–3%. However, there are side effects, including changes in periods (some women have sparse periods, others very heavy), spotting between periods, facial acne and painful breasts. There can also be a change in sexual desire, or it may cause an increase in appetite and weight gain, which can influence sexual behaviour as a secondary consequence. It is contraindicated for women with high blood pressure, diabetes, heart disease or depression.

The Ortho-Evra patch is a beige plastic patch that sticks to the stomach and releases synthetic oestrogen and progesterone for three weeks out of a four-week cycle. This patch prevents ovulation and also thickens cervical mucus, inhibiting the sperm. It is considered a highly effective method of contraception, and probably superior to the pill, although outcome studies have yet to be published. Combined hormone contraceptives have a slightly greater chance of serious blood-clotting conditions, especially if the woman is a smoker. Similar problems may occur with the Ring. The NuvaRing is a small flexible ring inserted into the vagina, which similarly releases synthetic oestrogen and progesterone. Again, no outcome studies have been published regarding its effectiveness, but there may be a danger of the ring slipping out of the vagina, and pregnancy could occur if it is not replaced within three hours. As with the patch, it is worn for three weeks out of a four-week cycle. It may cause an increase in weight and may also create vaginal irritation or infections.

Intrauterine devices (IUDs) are small T-shaped devices made of flexible plastic that contains a copper coil (ParaGard) or a hormone (Mirena). The coil can be left in place for twelve years and is thought to work by affecting how the sperm or egg moves. Mirena releases a small amount of progestogen, which thickens cervical mucus to prevent fertilization, and can last for five years. Both devices have a plastic string, which dangles into the vagina, that enables its removal. Both methods are thought to have a failure rate of less than 1%. Insertion, which is conducted by a clinician, may be painful, and the woman may experience backache for several weeks after. Occasionally, the uterus pushes the IUD out during a period. However, Mirena is ten times more expensive than the coil, despite its having fewer side effects such as weight gain or loss of libido, thus it may be less available in some areas of the country.

The most commonly used barrier method is the male condom, and less popular is the female condom. Condoms are sheaths of thin latex worn over the penis during intercourse. In addition to preventing fertilization, they are also effective in preventing the spread of sexually transmitted diseases. Condoms are considered to have a 15% failure rate as they may split or fall off during intercourse. More protection can be invoked by the additional use of a spermicide preparation. The female condom is a plastic pouch that sits inside the vagina with flexible rings at each end. The ring at the closed end holds the condom in place within the vagina, while the ring at the open end stays outside the vaginal opening. It is considered to have a 21% failure rate as they can rip or tear. The female condom is often used for protection during anal intercourse. Some men dislike the use of condoms as they feel it reduces their sensitivity. There may also be an inhibiting factor of having to stop foreplay during sexual behaviour to put it on.

Other barrier methods are diaphragms, caps and shields, which are silicone or soft latex barriers that cover the cervix and consequently block the opening to the uterus. They are used with a spermicidal cream that paralyzes the spermatozoa. These are considered to have a 6–16% failure rate as they can be pushed out of place by some sexual positions, can be difficult for a woman to insert and cannot be used during menstruation. They are less successful with women who have a poor vaginal tone or who suffer with frequent urinary tract infections. They are also contraindicated for women who have an allergy to latex, silicone or spermicide, or who have a history of toxic-shock syndrome.

Behavioural methods include the withdrawal approach and continuous abstinence. The withdrawal approach is when a man withdraws his penis from the vagina prior to ejaculation. The failure rate is quite high at 4–27% because pre-ejaculate leakage can contain sperm, and ejaculate on the vulval area can result in pregnancy. The advantage of this method is that there is no synthetic substance involved, so the natural hormones remain unaffected. However, the sexually inexperienced man, or a man who experiences premature ejaculation, should not use this method. He needs to be confident that he can identify the point of inevitability and to be able ejaculate well away from his partner's vagina. Continuous abstinence from sex may be an option for some couples, as there is a considerable proportion of people who are asexual. However, it is essential that both partners are willing participants in this policy; otherwise the relationship is doomed to fail.

Permanent methods of contraception involve the male having a vasectomy, as discussed in Question 6.6, or the woman having a tubal sterilization. For women who are very clear about not wanting any (further) children, this is a very effective method. It involves closing off the Fallopian tubes so that the ova and sperm cannot meet. As the woman's hormones are still produced, there are few side effects in terms of sexual desire, and this may have the effect of freeing a woman to express her sexuality more openly without fear of pregnancy. It has a 1% failure rate, and of these failures about a third may be ectopic pregnancies.

Thus, a couple wanting to prevent pregnancy have many options to choose from, but they all have some advantages and some disadvantages. No method is 100% safe (except celibacy). A knowledgeable counsellor can help a couple sort through a cost-benefit analysis to find the method that is appropriate for them.

CHAPTER 7

Discussing sex in the consulting room

7.1 When a couple never mention sex, I am not quite sure whether to ask any questions about it. Is this because sex is not an issue or because they are inhibited in talking about such intimate things? Is there a way of broaching the subject that is not intrusive?

Couples are increasingly seeking counselling help when an important relationship gets into trouble. If sex has become an obvious problem for them, they may seek out a qualified psychosexual therapist. Alternatively, they may go to a counsellor for couple therapy and may express their distress as a lack of communication, differences in upbringing or a lack of equality in the roles of the relationship. James and Wilson (1986) operationalized the work of couple therapy into the following list:

- establishing a working alliance
- working with communication
- changing behaviour through agreements
- creating therapeutic tasks
- recognition of mini and maxi problem areas

This is a useful working formulation of the work of couple counselling, irrespective of the therapeutic model of the counsellor.

If the couple attend counselling together for help when they are not getting on, it may be that they will not mention their sexual relationship to the counsellor either from embarrassment or because they may consider it inappropriate to discuss the most private aspect of their lives with an outsider. Yet it may be a fundamental area of dissatisfaction that can move from a mini to a maxi problem area. The frustration or lack of satisfaction in a sexual relationship can lead to displacement into other activities,

which might serve to increase the emotional space between the two partners. It is therefore the counsellor's role to introduce the subject, asking
pertinent questions in a matter-of-fact and explicit way, which in itself can
provide a role model for the couple to be open and frank in discussing any
sexual difficulties they may experience. The PLISSIT model (Annon, 1976)
was developed as a way of introducing communication about sex between
a clinician and a client (see Figure 7.1), and provides a progressive frame-
work for the counsellor to offer an approach that he or she can feel
comfortable with and competent in.

Permission giving	–	permission to talk about sex and maybe some reassurance that their behaviour or fears are normal
Limited Information	–	helping to dispel myths and misconceptions
Specific Suggestions	–	suggesting action steps, like recommending lubrication or medication
Intensive Therapy	–	referral to a psychosexual therapist

Figure 7.1 The PLISSIT model, after Annon, 1976.

For a counsellor, providing permission to talk about sex and offering
limited information is a valuable way of helping an inhibited client to move
forward without the counselling being considered too intrusive.

* * *

7.2 What specialist help is there for sexual problems? If a client of mine has such a problem, how do I find help for them, and should I stop seeing them in the meantime?

There is help available if a client confides that they are having sexual difficulties, both through the NHS and the private sector. The first port of call
should be the GP. Although many doctors are untrained in dealing with
sexual problems, and may not be able to offer help directly, sexual problems may be a symptom of an underlying physical illness, and this needs to
be discounted first. The GP is the gatekeeper of NHS referrals, and he or
she will then be able to refer the client on to a urologist, gynaecologist or
suggest a genito-urinary medicine clinic. Most of these clinics also have psychosexual nurses or psychosexual therapists attached to them to facilitate

an integration of therapeutic approaches between the medical and the psychological.

Should the client not wish to get help via the GP, help can be sought from a psychosexual therapist via the private sector. The client would be wise to choose a therapist who is accredited with the British Association for Sexual and Relationship Therapy (BASRT) or the Institute of Psychosexual Medicine (IPM), thus ensuring the standards of qualification and training of the therapist.

The counsellor should only continue seeing this client if there are issues outside of the sexual problem that need to be addressed.

* * *

7.3   I am a male counsellor, and I'm interested in undertaking training in psychosexual therapy. However, a female colleague advised me against it, as clients prefer to talk to female counsellors about sex problems. Is this really the case?

There are probably twice as many women therapists as there are men, and the reasons for this are complex. There are stereotypical differences in how men and women deal with emotional difficulties. Women are considered more verbal, more open to their feelings and more willing to discuss them. Men are considered to be more interested in problem-solving, less emotional and more rational. As Rose (2002) points out, men use 'report' talk whereas women use 'rapport' talk. She adds:

> To signal 'man', speak mainly of impersonal matters, be interested in information, value status, emphasise independence and be able to openly express aggression, competition and challenge. To signal 'woman', talk about personal issues, disclose, be attentive and sensitive to the needs of others and value intimacy and a sense of connectedness. (Rose, 2002: 8)

It is the feminine way of communicating that is considered to be the most appropriate for counselling, and yet it is this notion that provokes Rose to raise the intriguing question 'If we train men to be counsellors, are we requiring them not to behave as men?' Yet these traits are the stereotypical extremes of male and female communication, and, as has been discussed in Questions 2.3 and 2.4, masculinity and femininity are not mutually exclusive ends of a spectrum. There are many male therapists who are in touch with their feminine side and are able to be sensitive to the needs of their clients, while at the same time able to use their problem-solving skills to enhance the therapeutic work.

Research looking at the interaction between gender and the outcome of therapy shows little significant difference in outcome; and we know that it is not the gender of the therapist per se which is important in the outcome of good therapy but the therapeutic alliance between the counsellor and the client, irrespective of gender. In an interesting study by Ogrodniczuk et al. (2001), it was found that female clients preferred a form of supportive therapy that involved a collaborative relationship and problem-solving interventions, whereas male clients preferred a more interpretive form of therapy that encouraged introspection and examination of uncomfortable emotions. One could argue, therefore, that the preference is for the opposite-gender method of communication, as stereotypically men are thought to avoid uncomfortable emotions and women to avoid problem-solving and instead just want to talk.

In a survey conducted by Harris Interactive on behalf of *Psychology Today* (Singer et al., 2004), it was found that 58% of a large sample of men and women had no preference for a therapist's gender, 31% said they preferred a woman and 11% said they preferred a man. However, if the clients are lesbian or gay, they may view the gender (and, indeed, the sexuality) of the therapist more highly (Milton and Coyle, 1999). The results of this survey therefore suggest that 69% of their sample were more than happy to have a male therapist. Similarly, Glover and Wylie (1999) found that only 25% of clients would not accept a particular gender of a therapist when discussing sex problems. The male counsellor in this question should therefore go ahead with his proposed training, as the larger majority of clients would be prepared to see him. Nevertheless, since there is a minority of potential clients for whom gender is important, this is an issue that might need to be raised at assessment or at a first interview. Where there is any sign of hesitancy on the client's part, discussion on this issue can ascertain any concern about working with a counsellor who does not match the client's preference.

* * *

7.4 One of my clients fantasizes about having sex with me. Is this what is called an erotic transference? How can I best work with this without making the situation more difficult?

Freud (1915) was the first to write about the phenomenon of 'transference-love' between a therapist and a client after witnessing it between his close friend and colleague Joseph Breuer and the patient Anna 'O'. Freud conceptualized erotic transference as a manifestation of revisited past experiences, together with a strong resistance to the therapy. If the client can distract the therapist with protestations of love, the underlying work on the history is interrupted or avoided.

Over the years, opinion on the concept of erotic transference has been divided: *erotic transference* is thought to be a healthy love relationship that forms part of the therapeutic alliance and work, whereas *eroticized transference* is more severe, tenacious, and a delusional disturbance (Rappaport, 1956), which may manifest in inappropriate attachment within the therapy room, or stalking behaviours outside it.

With erotic transference, the therapeutic alliance per se promotes in some clients the need to love their therapist, particularly if they are dealing with attachment difficulties. It is through experiencing love for, and dependency on, the therapist that a client learns appropriate boundaries and develops autonomy outside the therapeutic frame with secure attachments.

Alternatively, eroticized transference involves an irrational preoccupation and idealization of the therapist, with demands for intimate or sexual fulfilment instead of therapy. Blum describes such a person as being 'flooded with erotic preoccupations and fantasies about the analyst' (Blum, 1973: 62). The client's attendance at therapeutic sessions serves only to allow closeness to the therapist, and not because the client wants to resolve difficult issues. Koo (2001) points out that in this situation the analytical situation reverses as the client tries to promote change in the therapist so that the proffered love will be acknowledged and accepted.

Much of the literature on erotic transference has focused on a female client with a male therapist, with little documentation written up by female therapists. Koo (2001) suggests that the reason for this is due to the social and political struggle for women to achieve a professional status. Writing about being treated as a sexual object by a client undermines that position. However, Person et al. (1993) point out that, if the situation is one of eroticized transference, the dyad is more likely to be that of an older male client with younger (often inexperienced) female therapist.

Contemporary theories underpinning erotic transference, while not disregarding Freud's view of therapeutic resistance, suggest that there may also be other issues that need to be considered. For some people who are insecurely attached, they may believe that they are so unlikely to be loved as they have had little or unpredictable experience of it that sex is the only way that they can get their intimacy needs met. Thus, in the intimacy of a therapeutic situation, the client might make sexual overtures as a way of getting close to a counsellor. Similarly, a male client may express sexual desires to a female therapist in preference to feeling the humiliation that might arise from expressing real fears about rejection or abandonment.

For a counsellor faced with the situation described in the question, an assessment needs to be made to determine whether it is a relatively benign erotic transference or the more difficult eroticized transference. It is preferable that this decision is made following discussion with the counsellor's supervisor, or with peers. If it is the former, sending the client away to another counsellor may damage the client further, as it taps into childhood fears of rejection and abandonment, and Rappaport (1956) believes that the client is likely to eroticize with the next counsellor anyway. It is preferable to maintain a steady relationship with the client, discussing the fantasies and what they may mean, without any breach of boundary or protocol on behalf of the counsellor. As House points out:

> ... the impulse to seek love is actually a healthy attempt at healing the early damage to the self that a pathological love environment precipitated in the first place. (House, 1996: 24)

He goes on to argue that feelings of love in therapy should be positively welcomed rather than resisted or defended against. So working through expressions of love or sexual fantasy can provide the client with a learning opportunity that he or she can have an intimate relationship without needing to be sexual.

It is a different situation with an eroticized transference, as working with such a client may lead to situations of harm to the therapist if the sexual demands are not met. I undertook a research study looking at such behaviour towards counsellors working in a primary-care setting (Hudson-Allez, 2002) and found that counsellors were twice as likely as the general population to have a situation of harassment or stalking from a current or former client who had developed an eroticized transference. The counsellor has to be very boundaried in this situation, as rejection of the client's sexual advances is likely to promote narcissistic rage (Meloy, 1998), which may put the counsellor in harm's way. Unless the counsellor has very good supervision and is strong enough to handle the intense feelings which are likely to be expressed, it is essential in this situation that the therapy is carefully terminated and that the client is referred for a psychiatric assessment.

* * *

7.5   I have seen a couple for therapy and find I am really attracted to the husband. He is very handsome, and I find myself wondering, as they talk about their sex lives, what it would be like to have sex with him. Should I stop seeing this couple?

Since the beginning of the talking cure in the early 1900s, there have been cases where therapists have entered into relationships with patients. Some such relationships have been notorious, like Jung's affair with Sabrina Spielrein. Most writers have warned against the potential for abuse in the power differential within the relationship. Other therapists have argued that it is a normal part of falling in love, much more than countertransference, and have married, as did the analyst Frieda Fromm-Reichman and her patient Erich Fromm, both of whom became very well-known analysts.

Person et al. (1993) identify four primary kinds of transference situations:

• heterosexual women in therapy with heterosexual male therapists
• heterosexual men in therapy with heterosexual female therapists
• homosexual men in therapy with homosexual male therapists
• homosexual women in therapy with homosexual female therapists

They point out that the last two categories have little literature to throw light upon the process.

Gabbard (1996) proposes two pathways whereby therapists might violate boundaries in therapeutic settings: through the 'lovesick therapist' or the 'masochistic surrender scenario'. The lovesick therapist is one whose own life and relationships are in disarray and so a pervasive role-reversal takes place in therapy. The counsellor starts to self-disclose, shifting the client into comforting the counsellor, as the focus of sessions starts turning away from the client and onto the therapist. Boundaries start to be eroded as time is extended, there are meetings outside of the therapy room, fees are dropped and touching begins. This scenario usually involves a male counsellor with a female client, although a male client with a cluster B personality disorder may occasionally draw in a female counsellor.

The masochistic surrender scenario is where the counsellor becomes so terrified that the patient may commit suicide that he or she becomes therapeutically ineffective. The client manipulates the counsellor sufficiently to believe that, unless his or her demands are met, the client will die and it will be entirely the counsellor's fault. The demands start as needy requests for attention but eventually become sexualized. Alternatively, the client may use what Person et al. (1993) call 'weak power', seducing the counsellor with appreciation, flattery and admiration.

Over the years of working within the profession, protocols regarding this behaviour in the codes of ethics of professional bodies have changed from the issue not being mentioned at all, to requiring a few months gap between the termination of therapy and before the commencement of a relationship, to the gap changing from months to years, to (in some institutions) a complete ban. Counsellors are very mindful of these therapeutic protocols and may feel uncomfortable with their own countertransference responses, fearing the reprobation of their peers. There are not many therapists like Field who are publicly willing to admit their own sexual arousal during therapy:

> . . . it was more than a response; it was as if her repressed desire . . . went
> directly into my unconscious and I assumed it was my own. (Field, 1996: 38)

There is disagreement in the literature cited by Field (1996) as to whether the therapist should share his or her countertransference feelings with the client. Some argue that it is vital for the healing of the patient for the therapist to acknowledge and own therapeutic feelings, whereas others warn against sharing this with the patient. Field offers an interesting compromise by pointing out that it is all right for a therapist to lose his heart, so long as he can still keep his head in maintaining the therapeutic commitment.

The counsellor in this question is experiencing an erotic countertransference to the husband. Essentially, there is nothing wrong with a healthy, erotic countertransference with an individual client. It demonstrates that the unconscious of the client is reaching the unconscious of the counsellor and that a therapeutic alliance has been formed. It can be therapeutically useful, providing that the therapist is aware of the situation, works with it consciously and is rigorous about maintaining boundaries. However, in this situation, the counsellor is seeing a couple, and such a dynamic may interfere with the objectivity of the client and bias the counsellor's approach in favour of the husband. The wife can soon recognize this and the couple work will be compromised.

Therefore, the counsellor needs to discuss with her supervisor her work with this couple and be open in supervision as to why she is fantasizing about having sex with this man. What is she missing in the couple work while she is thinking these thoughts? And, equally, what might she be missing in her own life and her own relationships? It will help if she investigates within supervision that she is making no deviations from her usual way of working and that her boundaries are clear. If the supervisor feels that the counsellor is blurring boundaries with the couple, and that this cannot be corrected, the therapy should be terminated and the couple referred on to another counsellor. An alternative explanation may be that the male client's feelings for the counsellor are intensely strong and are in part intended to seduce the counsellor away from examining his part in the couple dynamic, hoping that the counsellor will take his side against his partner. Countertransference responses can either be an indication of the counsellor's issue, the client's concern or more often a subtle blend of both, making disentangling what is happening within the counsellor of prime importance for the furtherance of the relationship with both partners.

CHAPTER 8
Variations in sexuality and gender

8.1 One of my clients who was sexually abused as a child is sure that this has made him a homosexual, yet he is turned off by the thought of sex with a man. Is the connection he has made a valid one? And is there any way of knowing whether he is homosexual or heterosexual?

As discussed in Question 8.4, homosexuality has been an ongoing fact of our evolutionary history, and evidence exists of its prevalence throughout the ancient civilizations. Research by Laumann et al. (1994) has found that the current prevalence rate of homosexuality in the States in men is 2.4% and 1.4% in women.

The question 'What causes homosexuality?' is fraught with political undertones as it implies that by understanding a 'cause' one is seeking the possibility of a 'cure'. The literature is rife with genetic, biosocial and neuroanatomical theories of why some people are gay. Sex with the same sex is not unknown in animal life, where it is called isosexuality: it is a common practice amongst fruit flies, whose DNA is very close to humans (Pattatucci and Hamer, 1995), pigeons, ravens, dolphins, chimpanzees, rhesus monkeys and bonobo apes, who use sex as an alternative to aggression (de Waal, 1995). It is known that homosexuality tends to run in families, and genes may play a part in this. However, despite many theories, no studies have found a gene for homosexuality, although it could be argued that there may be a genetic predisposition to homosexuality, and that, given certain triggers, it is more likely to occur in the children of homosexuals.

In a similar vein, LeVay (1991) found a difference in the size of the hypothalamus in the brains of heterosexual and homosexual men. He argues that men and women have different nuclei in their hypothalamus, which he

proposes might account for male-type behaviour. Thus, he feels he has provided a (tenuous) link, in that a male homosexual's brain is more like that
of a woman's. Once again, this very reductionist approach tries to simplify
the complexities of human behaviour. It is also criticized because it cannot
be determined whether any brain differences may be due to homosexual
differences or preferences rather than the other way round. It is known
that behaviour can change brain structure in the same way as brain structure can change behaviour (Schore, 1994). The gene theory is also an
attractive one for many to pursue, as it has been found that people who
believe in a genetic inheritability to homosexuality are less negative in their
attitudes towards them (Jayaratne, 2002).

Herdt (1990) categorizes cultural presentations of homosexuality as
follows:

- age-structured homosexuality: adolescent boys who perform fellatio
  with older men as part of a developmental progression – like the
  Ancient Greeks
- gender-reversed homosexuality: same-sex activity occurs as a result of
  cross-dressing and transgenderist activities
- role-specialized homosexuality: for cultures where homosexuality plays a
  social role, like shaman priests
- modern gay movement: in our society, homosexuality is not just behaviour but a political and social identity

Bem (1996) proposes a developmental theory he calls 'Exotic Become
Erotic' (EBE) as to why a person develops their own sexuality encompass-
ing the complexities of genes and culture. His proposal is that genes and
prenatal hormones create the antecedents not for sexual orientation but
for childhood temperaments that will predispose a child either to gender-
conforming or gender-nonconforming play behaviours. Feelings of
dissimilarity and unfamiliarity (exotic) with peers create non-specific autonomic arousal, which is later transformed into erotic arousal during
adolescence and adulthood. Thus, a child's being born a boy but with a
passive (feminine) temperament predisposes him to behave in gender-nonconforming ways, so he will feel more comfortable with girls who will play
in similar ways. When he mixes with masculine-type boys, he will feel alienated by their unfamiliarity and thus he will produce higher levels of
autonomic arousal in their presence, which in adulthood is turned into
erotic arousal and potential homosexuality.

There has been some evidence of a link between child sexual abuse and
homosexuality. Finkelhor (1984) found that, in a study of male college stu-
dents, those who had been abused in childhood by an adult were four times
more likely to be engaged in adult homosexuality. However, the reasons for
this finding are not that clear. Finkelhor suggests that these boys may have

been expressing early homosexual interest and curiosity and thus placing themselves in a position of vulnerability from predatory males. Jehu (1988) also proposes that these boys may have labelled themselves as a consequence of the abuse because they did not resist the advances or may have experienced physical pleasure during the abuse. If this pre-labelling has occurred, these boys are more likely to adopt the role and lifestyle of a homosexual.

The client in this question has been sexually abused as a child, and still clearly has issues that need to be resolved in therapy. It is essential that the counsellor encourage the client to discuss the detail of the abusive experiences as a necessary component of the recovery process (Burke Drauker, 1992). As with this client, it is not unusual for a client who has been the victim of same-sex abuse to believe that the pleasure he experienced during the activity represents latent homosexual desires (Struve, 1990). As the counsellor works with a client through the abusive issues, reframing these normal childhood physical responses to sexual stimulation, the client can be helped to reach an understanding that even though his body responded to the abusive activity this does not mean that he sought it or that he enjoyed it. It is wise, therefore, for the counsellor to avoid any focus of the bipolar concept of sexuality in the early stages of the therapeutic encounter. As Mustanski and Bailey (2003) argue, a client who struggles with the origin of his or her sexual orientation is focusing on the wrong issue. Work of more value will be conducted in therapy by encouraging self-acceptance, no matter what the orientation.

* * *

8.2 One of my female clients says she enjoys sex with men and with women equally. I know Freud thought we are all bisexual, but since she says she wants to settle down in a long-term relationship is there any way I can help her decide whether it is to be with a man or a woman?

Bisexuals are attracted to either sex as partners, and, as discussed in Question 8.1, there is no specific predetermination for an individual's sexual orientation. Freudian theory proposed that an infant was polymorphously perverse and was able to direct his or her sexuality to a variety of objects (Tollison and Adams, 1979). Harlow (1971) also proposes an inherent bisexuality within our species after his extensive primate research. He argues:

> Bisexual potential is a fact in humans and in monkeys, and judgement of any sex-role behaviour as normal or abnormal is only in relation to some man-made standard, real or fictitious. (Harlow, 1971: 93)

Bisexuals may choose relationships with men and women at the same time, or may alternate with serial monogamy. They seem to offer their partners either passion or nurturing (Love, 1992).

In Question 2.1, it was proposed that gender is neither a male nor a female phenomenon but a spectrum between the two. Similarly, sexuality may also fit in a spectrum, and many people, if they dare admit it, have experienced both heterosexual and homosexual feelings at some time during their lives. Some people openly say that they enjoy sexual activity with both sexes, terming themselves as bisexual, but the majority of people, perhaps after testing the water during transitional phases in their lives, settle down at one end or the other of the spectrum. Fausto-Sterling (1992) highlights this proposed spectrum admirably as she expresses her exasperation with LeVay (see Question 8.1), who believed he had found the biological determinant of human sexual behaviour:

> The LeVay study confounds sex and gender . . . How can he explain the football hero – masculine to the core – who is nevertheless gay? And what about the highly feminine lesbian, the straight man who fantasizes about having sex with a man while making love to his wife or who experiences sexual excitement from anal penetration, the lesbian who fantasizes about penile penetration while making love to her lady friend, or the well-known phenomenon of situational homosexuality that occurs in institutions such as prison? The examples reiterate that human sexuality is not an either/or proposition. (Fausto-Sterling, 1992: 249)

Baumeister (2004) points out some heterosexual women may begin to experiment with lesbian activities in their thirties and forties, and equally some lesbian women may start having sex with men after years of same-sex orientation, suggesting sexual plasticity.

As suggested in the last question, therefore, when working with a client who is unsure of her sexuality at the present time, the focus of the work should not be on the presentation of her sexuality per se, or whether she should be with a man or a woman, but on making her feel comfortable with herself and with other people, allowing her to fall in love naturally and choose when she wants to make a relationship whether is be with a man or a woman.

* * *

8.3 I've noticed as a heterosexual working with some gay male clients that their sexual relationships sometimes seem to be more casual than the relationships of most of my heterosexual clients. Are there different sexual habits and different sexual practices that I don't understand or maybe am intolerant towards?

Gay lifestyles, on the whole, are very similar to heterosexual lifestyles. Many form long and loving partnerships and remain monogamous. Gay men have benefits that heterosexual couples may not have: a double male income, a deeper understanding of the psychology of their partner and a common bond of adversity in the sometimes negative responses of the society that surrounds them. Lesbians have an advantage over men in a relationship, as one of the partners will be able to have children with the aid of a donor male friend, although their income level will invariably be different. Some of these couples have very full sex lives; others choose not to be sexual at all.

Having said that, there are some gay men who participate in anonymous sexual activity outside of their relationships. This may occur in public toilets (known as cottaging), in public parks or other areas known to the gay community, on trains, in cafés or tearooms. Many participate in such sexual activity without speaking, in some cases even without seeing their partner's face through strategically positioned holes in cubicle walls. Some of these men may be openly gay and involved in the gay community. Others may be married, having a sexual relationship in the marriage that may or may not be fulfilling, but who choose to keep their homosexuality a well-guarded secret.

It has been established that there is a correlation between homosexuality in men and an increase in depression, anxiety and suicidal behaviour (Gilman et al., 2001). Although the reasons for this are not clear, this may be due to stigma or the social vulnerability of the threat of HIV. Bancroft et al., (2003b) suggest that some of these men have an increase of sexual activity as they become anxious or depressed and may then adopt more risky-sex behaviour, in particular over the use of condoms. They point out that this 'what the heck' phenomenon is particularly noticeable in gay men and may indicate a sense of fatalism in their sexual risk-taking (see also Kalichman et al., 1997).

Counsellors working with this client group need to be clear about their own feelings toward a client's behaviour, especially when it demonstrates a different value system to their own. There are few gay men or lesbian women who have not experienced some form of homophobia at some point in their lives; so it is important that counsellors examine their own potentially homophobic feelings, and perhaps investigate such anxieties or desires in their own personal therapy. Many gay and lesbian clients prefer to seek gay or lesbian counsellors, in the hope that their position and values will be better understood.

* * *

8.4   A rather rigid Christian I am seeing has been told by her son that he is gay. She is convinced there is a connection between male homosexuality and paedophilia. How do I convince her otherwise?

It is not surprising that people make a link between homosexuality and paedophilia as such a link goes back to the Ancient Greeks. In those times, it was normal for a man to practise both homosexuality and paedophilia, even though he was married and rearing children. Greek men had boys for sexual pleasure as a contraceptive measure, as it allowed their wives respite while they went about the business of child rearing. The boys (catamites) were also expected to be sexual with mentors or teachers, and a boy of any breeding would not be considered to have completed education unless he had an adult male lover, almost like a rite of passage (Schlegel, 1995). However, this homosexuality with boys and adolescents was essentially a transient behaviour because as the boys became men they would marry and have children.

Despite this ancient practice, contemporary research literature demonstrates that there is little correlation between homosexuality and paedophilia, and there is no reason to suggest that homosexuals are any more likely to become sexually involved with children than heterosexuals (Howitt, 1995). Indeed, some studies have suggested the opposite, that unless a male homosexual has a history of offending against children, he is unlikely to offend against children under any circumstances (Groth, 1979).

It is not a counsellor's role to convince clients that they are wrong in their belief system, but imparting knowledge and understanding may be helpful in this case. Since this client is fearful about what her son might do, it might also be helpful to encourage her to review her relationship with her son, her memories of his upbringing and the lessons she taught him over his childhood years, lest she thinks she contributed in any way to his stated sexuality. That way she may be able to convince herself that neither she nor anyone else has harmed her son's sexual development, which in turn may contribute to dissolving some of her fears about him.

* * *

8.5 I have a client who likes to dress up in women's clothes, but he denies that he wants to become a woman. What is the difference between transvestites and men who want to change sex?

The language of 'trans' is new and still evolving, and, as much as any minority group, transvestites hate to be categorized. But for the counsellor who needs to distinguish between different terms, there are:

- *cross-dressers, transvestites, or TVs*: these individuals may include people who cross-dress privately or even in secret, those who have come out into the public arena and those who do so for remuneration, like drag kings and queens. Most cross-dressers are heterosexual and do not want to change sex, even if those offended by their behaviour may feel it would be easier and better if they would.
- *transsexuals, or TSs*: these are men or woman who change their biological sex to fit in with their perceived gender identity. A transsexual, whose perception and identification is completely within the opposite role, often has a sexual desire towards people within the same gender as they were born. Transsexuals do not perceive themselves as homosexual, although outsiders may.
- *transgenderists, TGs, or gender-fuckers*: these are individuals who mix (or transgress) their gender identity and gender presentation. For example, a large male biker with full hairy beard and wearing a mini-skirt and high heels. Transgenderists often transcend the limits of sexuality too, and many tend to be bisexual.
- *intersexuals*: those born with both biological sexes (see Question 8.8).

Cross-dressers enjoy wearing the clothing of the opposite biological sex. Those who are most noticed are heterosexual men who enjoy wearing women's clothing, since after the rise of feminism, women have worn men's suits, ties etc. without attracting significant attention. Cross-dressing occurs either for personal or professional satisfaction, for sexual arousal and gratification or for comfort and relaxation. The majority of such men feel comfortable in their gender roles but not in their gender identity and prefer to be considered as androgynous. They are not necessarily homosexual, and many enjoy loving relationships with their wife or female partner even though at times they wear women's clothing.

The DSM IV (1994) (302.3) has a category called 'transvestic fetishism', which describes a heterosexual male who becomes sexually aroused by cross-dressing, and where these sexual urges or fantasies create emotional distress or impair social or occupational functioning. This person, when not cross-dressed, is masculine and usually heterosexual. There may also be the association of sexual masochism in the behaviour. Often this form of cross-dressing develops in early adolescence and is conducted in secret, used as a stimulus to masturbation (Rowe, 1997), although it is not clear whether this is a compulsion or an irresistible desire. In such a case, the individual becomes both the object and the subject of his sexual fantasy (Harris, personal communication, 2000), and in many cases the cross-dressing becomes a coping strategy to deal with feelings of anxiety or depression.

Some researchers try to relate transsexualism to homosexuality (Blanchard et al., 1985) and have tried to classify them accordingly into:

- Androphile – a young person who objects to his or her biological sex. These individuals are seen as acting outside expected gender roles from early years and are usually regarded as homosexual. Sometimes called a 'true transsexual'.
- Autogynophile – these people have gender-typical childhoods. Difficulties crop up later in life and often start through getting sexually aroused by cross-dressing and images of women. They are seen as a fetishistic transvestite.

These ideas are not accepted by trans society. It is extremely rare to find a true transsexual under this definition, and most transsexuals will present with a history of adolescent fetishistic cross-dressing either in fantasy or reality.

Transgenderists are those who feel that their gender identity is the opposite of their biological sex. They do not necessarily *want* to be someone of the opposite gender, but feel that is what they are: trapped inside the wrong body. They often behave in ways that make them feel more comfortable with their felt sense, or at least as far as they think society will allow. So, for example, a transgendered man may wear female underwear, tights and skirts in his own home but will not do so at work for fear of reprisals. Transgendered men can be more androgynous and can therefore be more accepting, but those with whom they relate may well ask themselves 'Is this person I am talking to a man or a woman?' Counsellors can experience this dilemma, when they are unsure whether to call the client a man or a woman. There may also be differences in societal sub-cultures in how transgenderists are received. A transgendered man may be more accepted in a lesbian society, whereas a transgendered woman may find herself more accepted within the gay community. Not all transgenderists wish to, or are able to, undergo sexual reassignment surgery (SRS). However, they may feel they want the support of others with similar issues; the Beaumont Society, founded for such people, currently has over 800 members.

Elkins (1997) identifies five stages that an M2F individual goes through, in a process he calls male-femaling:

- beginning – usually private experiences of dressing
- 'fantasying' – simple and elaborate fantasies of being female
- doing – acting out in mannerisms and dress
- constituting – fitting the female activities into his life
- consolidating – finding a way of being that fits and works by choosing one of the following modes of male-femaling:

  - aparting – maintaining the boundaries of gender
  - substituting – increasingly female takes over the male
  - integrating – transcending conventional models and transgressing stereotypes

Elkins points out that the whole process is one of construction and reconstruction for the development of schema that are consistent with how she perceives herself to be.

For a client presenting with transgender issues, it may be useful to discuss the different types of presentation and ask the client how he or she perceives himself or herself. However, it may be that such clients move through these different categories and back again during the course of therapy, and during the course of their life. Istar Lev (2004) has produced very comprehensive guidance for working with gender-variant people and their families.

* * *

8.6 One of my clients has been accepted for surgery to change his sex. He tells me he is having some counselling in connection with this. What will happen to him, what sort of counselling will he be having and how might that affect the way I work with him in therapy?

Some transgendered individuals get to a stage where they feel they can no longer maintain what they experience as the façade of being the wrong person in the wrong body and they decide to come out. They adopt a new name, a more open way of cross-dressing, sometimes changing their occupation and trying to live as the person they want to become. This is called transitioning, and part of this process may involve applying for sexual reassignment surgery (SRS).

It may be assumed that there are more M2F than F2M transsexuals, as there are far fewer surgical procedures conducted on F2M. However, more often than not, hormone therapy alone is sufficient for an F2M, therefore surgery is not considered so essential. The cost of F2M surgery is also prohibitive and often has a less-successful outcome, although there have been great surgical advancements in the development of phalloplasty. Studies tend to suggest that F2M transsexuals form more stable partnerships after SRS, accept their new role more readily, are more likely to be exclusively heterosexual (Pauly, 1974) and are usually fully accepted by their female partner. Pauly describes them as 'better adjusted, freer of paranoid trends, and more realistic in their appraisal of what is possible for them'.

Dr Harry Benjamin was the medical endocrinologist and sexologist who pioneered the surgery for transsexuals and developed the currently accepted protocols for the surgical procedures (Benjamin, 1966).

If the client has applied for SRS on the NHS, (there are three principal Gender Identity Clinics within the UK), there will be a life-test requirement of living in the new identity for at least two years (one year if the person goes for private treatment), and two psychiatric referrals, before hormones are prescribed prior to SRS. There is also a requirement of a minimum of three months psychotherapy before hormone treatment or any other procedure like speech therapy is initiated. The psychiatric referral is necessary as some forms of schizophrenia and similar delusional conditions can mimic transsexualism.

At the start of the real life test (RLT), the person changes his or her name by statutory declaration or deed poll and is given new NHS papers amending their gender in the records. Under the Gender Recognition Act of 2004, the person can apply for a gender-recognition certificate after a two-year transition, even if they have not undergone SRS. This certificate will allow the person to acquire a new birth certificate, to apply for a passport and to marry under the new gender. The RLT can produce difficulties per se as it involves the person using the toilets, changing rooms and other facilities of their felt gender. He or she therefore has to withstand challenges and discrimination as they try to 'pass' or gain acceptance in their chosen identity. Particular difficulties arise in passing, not only because of voice pitch or facial hair, but also in getting the nuance of mannerisms, vocabulary and personality right. It is also fair to say that a transgenderist has to work a lot harder to appear male or female than an individual who is already biologically in that role, where ambiguity is somewhat taken for granted.

Counselling at this stage may be in a gender-identity clinic, where there will be coaching for the individual in stereotypical ways that men or women walk, talk, dress etc. There is a requirement that the transgenderist can fit into the stereotypical role in order to be accepted for the medical treatment. Ambiguity or androgyny is not encouraged. Western society enforces a choice of bipolar extremes, whereas in Eastern philosophies, like Buddhism, people are encouraged to seek a middle path.

A transsexual woman (that is an M2F) can expect to receive large doses of oestrogens with some progestogens that will reduce the size of her penis and scrotum; the prostate will atrophy, her skin will soften and her body shape will change redistributing facial and body fat and enhancing the breast area and enlarging the areola. The hair will improve in strength and condition, although treatment will not change a receding hair line. Breast growth can be augmented surgically and with an increased use of progestogen. There may also be some concomitant anti-androgen treatment to reduce the effect of the testosterone. Hormones will not raise her voice or reduce her facial hair; so she will need to opt for expensive laser or electrolysis treatments to be a convincing female. The penis may atrophy; so there will be a continuing need to keep stretching the skin in order to retain its elasticity, as this will be used for the creation of the vagina. Little is known about the long-term effects of hormone supplementation, although the risks of a deep-vein thrombosis or pulmonary embolism are increased, especially if the person is overweight or a smoker. The hormone treatment is discontinued three to six weeks prior to surgery to reduce the likelihood of a thrombo-embolic event.

The primary surgery for an M2F involves the removal of the testes by orchidectomy and using the skin of the penis, which is turned inside out, to construct a vaginal passage (vaginoplasty). There may also be breast augmentation using silicone implants and an 'Adam's shaving' to reduce the size of the thyroid cartilage. Secondary procedures may involve vaginal lengthening, labioplasty to create labia and a clitoridoplasty to form a clitoris. This surgery is painful, and as with any surgery carries its own risks of post-operative infections. There may also be post-operative genito-urinary infections like candidiasis (thrush). The results are also unpredictable, as in vaginoplasty, fistulae may form between the vagina and rectum. Scar tissue may also interfere with urination. As discussed in Question 8.8 on intersex, there may also be difficulties with colovaginoplasty procedures, where a piece of the colon is grafted for the vagina, as some of these patients experience a painful spasm either during or after intercourse. There is also an increased risk of cancer with this procedure, although cervical screening is not conducted on M2Fs, as it is argued that they do not possess cervical tissue, the apex of the vaginal opening being closed off with penile or scrotal material. However, screening is standard practice in the United States.

Hormone treatment for F2M consists of increased testosterone, which stops the pituitary production of ovarian activity and thus terminates menstruation. Testosterone will also enlarge the clitoris and increase the appetite and libido. The voice will break irreversibly, and the rate of hair growth will increase, which can be enhanced by repetitive shaving. This may produce a side effect of acne. This hormone treatment for all transsexuals is a life-long procedure.

Surgery for an F2M transsexual is fraught with difficulties, and the outcome is usually poor. If the person wants a full penis to have penetrative sex, he will require a phalloplasty. This may be created using penile prostheses and skin grafts. There are two sorts of prostheses: the cheaper version consists of two malleable rods, as used for men with permanent erectile failure. This gives a semi-erect enduring protrusion. Alternatively, the more upmarket version is a prosthesis with a pump that sits inside the scrotum, allowing the man to pump it up and down at will. Some men opt not to go for the full phalloplasty, as the results are variable. Instead, they may choose to have a urethral extension to the clitoris (which will have enlarged with the testosterone supplementation), so that they can urinate in a standing position. In addition to the phalloplasty, common requirements are a scrotoplasty and double mastectomy. Secondary surgery may involve having a hysterectomy and oophorectomy, although these are not essential, as they no longer function.

Assuming the counselling this client is having is pre-hormonal therapy, the work undertaken by the questioner may be more supportive during the process of change. Supporting the person through his or her own issues and experiences so that he or she feels clear about the decision and consequences of undergoing SRS can be very beneficial. It is also helpful to encourage the person not to see reassignment surgery as the ultimate goal, in the hope that everything thereafter will just fall into place. Experience suggests it will not; so his or her overarching goal needs to be the successful passing from one gender to another without challenge or ridicule from outsiders. A good question to ask a transsexual client is 'If the gender reassignment surgery could never take place, would you still choose to live as a woman (or man)?'

Transsexuals, as a result of their gender dysphoria, are also often severely depressed and express feelings of helplessness and persecution. If the transsexual was married, there are often difficulties within the relationship, as the partner has to make a decision as to whether he or she wants to stay with the transformed person. If the partnership fails, grief work for the losses incurred may be valuable. Other members of his or her family may also react strongly: children, parents, close friends etc. Their reactions may invoke strong feelings of shame, guilt, loss, anger or incredulity.

Furthermore, if surgery is not offered, there is a high risk of suicidal behaviour, making for another important issue that needs to be discussed and, where possible, worked through.

* * *

8.7 If my client changes from a man to a woman through surgery but still loves and wants a sexual relationship with his wife, does that mean he is homosexual?

Transgendered men and women may be heterosexual, bisexual, lesbian or gay, as much as any other individual. However, in the process of changing their gender, some people around them may deny their gender identity. For example, a man who has changed into a woman may well view herself as heterosexual because she is interested in the opposite sex, that is men. Other people, however, may accuse her of being gay, as they do not accept that inside she always felt female; they only see her previously external masculinity.

Griggs (1998) discusses how the experience of transsexualism throws our understanding of sexuality into chaos. Does one describe a transgenderist whose gender identity and presentation is female but still has male genitals as male or female in determining whether his or her sexual desires towards a man are heterosexual or homosexual? And what if the man of these desires is an F2M transsexual? Griggs argues that we need something more than body morphology to make that determination, and that cognitive processes here are essential. This suggests that the greatest sexual organ is within the brain!

Very often some individuals going through sexual reassignment have no real sense of what their sexuality is going to be until they get there. When a person is going through a metamorphosis, sometimes it is necessary to emerge from the chrysalis and let their wings dry before they know in which direction they want to fly. Until such time, the prevailing priority is the felt gender identity and biological sex realignment.

* * *

8.8   My client was born with both male and female genitalia. The penis was removed at birth, and she was brought up as a woman. She says she feels increasingly more distressed about this, saying they made the wrong decision. How can I help my client make a decision about her gender?

A child born with both male and female genitalia is considered hermaph-rodite, named after the Greek myth of Hermaphroditus, who was the son of Hermes and Aphrodite who merged with the nymph Salmacis to form one body. The term hermaphrodite is now considered pejorative and stig-matizing. However, in contemporary society, intersex, as it is now called, is still little accepted and rarely discussed.

Modern science now informs us that there are many as 30 different gene disorders causing disordered sexual development in humans, not counting hypothalamic or pituitary causes. These are some of the syndromes that can lead to intersex babies:

- *Problems in the genes*: 46XY female (female appearance with a male kary-otype) or 46XX male (male appearance with female karyotype), Turner syndrome (ovarian failure), Klinefelter syndrome (testicular failure)
- *Problems with the gonads*: gonadal digenesis (mutations or no gonads), congenital androgen insufficiency syndrome (CAIS), true hermaphro-ditism (with the individual having a testicle on the right side and an ovary on the left, extremely rare)
- *Problems with the genitals*: micropenis (see Question 2.5), hypospadias, cli-toromegaly.

The most-common response by medical practitioners in these circum-stances is to make a decision on the basis of the visible genitalia and chromosomal determination. The medical practitioners, who feel they are acting in the best interests of the child by choosing the gender commen-surate to the best outcome of surgical procedures, would lead shocked parents into making gender-assignment decisions. Before the days of ultra-sound scanning, this may have meant a surgical procedure to open up the abdomen to determine whether the child had a uterus or not. If there was no uterus, any vaginal opening and visible labia would be removed, high doses of testosterone prescribed and the child reared as a boy. If there was a uterus, the extended clitoris would have been reduced or removed (cli-toridectomy), together with vaginoplasty to create a vaginal passage or to gain access to an existing vaginal passage already high in the pelvis. Sometimes the surgeon would use existing tissue for this; sometimes they would take a section of the colon or rectum. The created vaginal passage has a propensity to seal over, however, so the child and adolescent would be expected to insert vaginal trainers daily until she had a regular sexual partner. Scarring was also an ongoing problem in terms of sensitivity or pain, asymmetrical labia and abnormal appearance. Some would be left horribly mutilated, and intersex women reported problems such as vaginal stenosis, genital pain, anorgasmia and impaired or complete loss of genital sensation.

Modern-day surgical procedures are much improved, and the decision or choice of gender may be made on the basis of chromosomal markers and on potential fertility as well as external genitalia appearance. The surgery may need to be repeated throughout the development of the child, as well as the additional use of hormones to reinforce the chosen gender. Contemporary methods of medical intervention have advanced, of course. Some intersex babies are discovered during the course of ultra-sound scanning and may be determined visually as early as ten to eleven weeks' gestation. For example, if the penile protrusion points upwards, that is considered to be a normal phallus. If it points downwards, that may indicate an extended clitoris. Amniocentesis may also give an indication of sexual abnormalities. Trials are currently being undertaken to commence treatment for this as early as five weeks' gestation using Dexamethasone, although there is no data yet on the long-term outcome for either the infant or the mother. Contemporary surgery is also conducted much more sensitively. Surgeons have been persuaded to be less aggressive with clitoral surgery, by reducing the erectile tissue while leaving the neuronal pathways and clitoral hood intact. Interestingly, however, it is known that, even after a clitoral reduction, in one-quarter of cases the tissue may regrow to its original size. Modern surgeons are also likely to review an infant who has received such surgery again at aged ten to check for any potential problems prior to menstruation, and similarly again at age sixteen prior to sexual intercourse.

Not all intersex individuals are diagnosed in infancy. There may have previously been no external sign of intersex at birth, as the dual organs may have been internal, but, as puberty is reached, hormonal changes occur and the differences may become more pronounced. For example, a clitoris may start to extend into a penis. This may be indicative of testicular feminizing syndrome (TFS) or congenital androgen insensitivity syndrome (CAIS). With these conditions there may be no indication until an adolescent girl is investigated for not menstruating or for infertility, only to find that she is genetically male and possesses a shortened vagina, no uterus and internal, undescended testes. Money (1972) studied ten women with

TFS and found that although they were genetically male, eight preferred to be female and all of them dreamed about raising children. This suggests that socialization of gender can be a stronger predeterminer of gender identity than biological sex.

However, medical criteria are not the only influences determining whether an infant with ambiguous genitalia is raised as male or female. There are also cultural factors that influence the decision. In the Western world, the default position for raising an intersex baby has been female, as it is perceived that female genitalia are easier to construct than male. In Malaysian Muslims, there is a similar default, because women inherit property. In China, and other countries, the preference may be for a male. So, as well as medical reasons for the choice, there are cultural, political and religious pressures that may influence the decision as to what sex the child is raised. In Question 2.3, I give the example of the Berdache of the American Indians and their openness to changing gender. Similarly, in Papua New Guinea there is an acceptance and recognition of a third gender, and changing from one to the other is accepted. We may want to consider whether, if our Western society had never developed the medical and surgical interventions that assign an intersex to one sex or the other, our society would have grown more tolerant of ambiguity and difference and would have been prepared to consider gender as a continuum rather than as a bipolar concept.

One of the first questions asked at the birth of a child is 'Is it a girl or a boy?' It is a clear 'either/or' question, so a response of 'Both' or 'I'm not sure' would be met with a stunned silence, disapproval or even disgust. As a result, there has often been secrecy surrounding these surgical procedures, encouraged by the medical profession, who feared that knowledge of their diagnosis would lead people to suicide. Parents and family might tell as few people as possible, knowing that the child could be taunted and alienated by children and adults alike. The secret may be held so tightly that even the child would not be told and may only find out by accident in adulthood. Thus, the child would be left to struggle through the turbulent developmental emotions that would occur, particularly at the pubescent stage. Such secrecy creates difficulties. Often these children are advised by their parents never to undress in front of their peers in case differences or surgical scars are observed. This creates a feeling of shame and abhorrence regarding one's own body. It also makes others more curious and more likely to want to see – bringing about what is trying to be avoided. All this, together with the prohibition on talking and discussing their differences, leaves these children more vulnerable to predatory adults and for abuse to occur. For a child who has been brought up to hide and abhor their genitalia, sexually abusive behaviour can feel comforting and rewarding; here is someone who is enjoying what they have, rather than telling them to hide and not talk about it.

With modern medical methods, requirements for consent to treatment and patient access to medical notes, it is now considered inappropriate not to tell the parents and the child when he or she was old enough regarding the condition. But there is still controversy over whether the parents and the surgeon have the right to determine an infant's sex and undertake irreversible surgery, thus taking away the individual's right to choose at a later date. An interesting anomaly of the law is that since 1985 there has been a law prohibiting female genital mutilation, but this does not apply to intersex individuals. Since the cosmetic-outcome evidence-base for surgery on infants is slim, the long-term psychosocial and psychosexual development has not been enhanced and these patients as adults have expressed deep dissatisfaction with the procedures undertaken, it is perhaps time to review the efficacy of performing sexual reassignment surgery (SRS) on infants at all, and instead give parents social and psychological support to help them cope with their infant when perceived as different.

Some intersexuals are happy with the sex assigned to them and have a similar gender identity to match, and therefore do not wish to change it. Others, however, are resentful at the sex they feel has been imposed on them by outsiders and may develop gender dysphoria. Surgery may remove visible signs of the alternative gender, but internally and hormonally the person may always feel either male or female, or both male and female, and it is at this stage that the individual may become distressed. If the person is not aware of their own history of gender reassignment, this may manifest in acting out, mood swings and confusion regarding their sexuality. Knowledge of their history and the procedures undertaken without their consent may similarly bring swings of rage and grief for their lost body parts and parts of themselves. Surgery without psychological support may also reinforce feelings of inadequacy and abnormality.

These then, are some of the issues an intersex person will bring to the counselling room:

• Who or what am I?
• Why was I not told?
• Why me?
• Who should I tell?
• What pronoun should I use to describe myself?
• Can I ever have a loving relationship?
• Can I have children?
• I want to have 'normal' penetrative sex
• How can I determine my sexuality?

The counsellor needs to be open to these issues, on the premise that gender is not bipolar and that a person does not have to be 'him' or 'her'; rather, the client may be able to decide which gender to choose. The client may even go for the option of staying as both and accepting and liking themselves just as they are. It is also helpful to encourage the person to think beyond the stereotypical concept of sexual activity, that womanhood does not necessarily mean the ability to be penetrated or that manhood does not have to mean the ability to penetrate. Counselling may be able to help the client to view themselves as an individual, both unique and yet also like others, rather than as someone who continues to pathologize themselves, as the doctors may have done, as abnormal.

This is not to ignore the fact that such clients may exhibit trauma behaviours, as ongoing medical examinations can feel abusive to a young child. There may also be a sense that as they have had so many genital examinations, their body does not belong to them, and that it belongs as much to the doctors. In these situations, it can be very difficult to be sexual with another person. Counselling can therefore assist such clients to deal with the trauma of the past, to take ownership of their bodies and to foster their ability to express themselves sexually.

CHAPTER 9

Sexual diversity

9.1 I have been asked to help a man who downloads pictures from the Internet and is afraid he is a paedophile. Is there a close connection between looking and doing? And can I, without specialist knowledge, be of any help to him?

To answer this question fully, it is necessary to look at this client's use of the Internet – is it a problem? In a classic study by Cooper et al. (1999) of 10,000 men and women in an admitted, non-random, self-selecting sample, 15–20% of Internet users said they engaged in some form of sexual activity on the Net (cybersex), with 8% showing signs of sexual compulsivity. Interestingly, a gender difference was found in that men accessed erotica and porn, whereas women accessed chat rooms to build sexual relationships. This mirrors the arousal systems discussed in answers to other questions, where men are very visual with their sexual arousal, whereas women are cognitive and interested in relationships. Thirty-two percent of the sample acknowledged that their activity jeopardized at least one important area of their life. Twenty percent of men and 12% of women admitted using their work computer for some form of sexual activity, with 70% of Internet pornography traffic occurring between the hours of 9 a.m. and 5 p.m.

So why do people get so involved in Internet sexual activity? Cooper (1998) proposes what he calls the Triple 'A' engine:

- Affordability – based on supply and demand; there are many sites because lots of people want to access them
- Accessibility – people can satisfy every sexual need without having to delay gratification
- Anonymity – allows gratification without personal disclosure

105

In addition, Ross and Kauth (2002) add another two 'A's to the standard Triple 'A', calling it the Quin-A engine, when referring to men who have sex with men:

* Acceptability – certainly within the gay culture
* Approximation – it allows men to test out their sexuality through fictitious selves or virtual sex; this can be considered a useful therapeutic tool for those who have doubts or fears regarding their sexuality

Carnes et al. (2001) distinguish between various categories of cybersex user, rather than considering it a unitary concept:

* *Appropriate recreational users* – those who engage in cybersex with no adverse consequences
* *Inappropriate recreational users* – those who are not necessarily compulsive but use sexual information at inappropriate times (like at work) or with inappropriate people (like colleagues) to gain attention
* *Discovery group* – here the Internet becomes the trigger for compulsive sexual behaviour
* *Predisposed group* – those who had previous compulsive problems with minor sexual fantasies or behaviours
* *Life-long sexual compulsives* – those who experience lifelong struggles with problematic compulsive sexual behaviour

There are three further sub-types that need to be considered when undertaking an assessment of the pathology of the Internet user:

* *Stress reactive* – those who use the Internet to relieve high levels of stress
* *Depressive* – where the Net becomes an escape from depression
* *Fantasy* – as an escape from the dull routine of life into sexual fulfilment

It is essential to make an assessment of the client. Not all sexual encounters on the Internet are negative; some people have been able to develop sexually, buy sexual aids and meet sexual partners via their computer. It has provided a positive outlet for the disenfranchized, like people with disabilities, to explore their sexuality. And most people experience few problems with their Internet usage. However, a minority (1%) have a serious problem with it and spend more than forty hours each week on online sexual activities.

The Internet has the ability to provide previously unseen visual information, which creates such high levels of arousal that it invokes a conditioned physiological response, together with a psychological need for more. It had been previously held that a person's sexuality was laid down between five and eleven years old in an arousal template or lovemap (Money, 1986). Yet, with the use of the Internet, patients report becoming obsessed with images and behaviours that they were not aware of until they were, for example, in their sixties and began using their computer. These users experience high degrees of arousal, which they are unable to stop, with no prior history of compulsive sexual behaviour. This goes counter to the literature that advocates the basis for obsessional sexual behaviour developed as a result of early childhood abuse.

As the client in this question is fearful that his behaviour makes him a paedophile, he is clearly looking at sexual pictures of children. Paedophilia networks have been using the Internet since 1985 (Akdeniz, 1999). The search for solutions to child porn started in the UK in 1995 with the police's Operation Starburst, but more recently Operation Ore has brought a lot of Internet users to the surface, some seeking therapeutic help. This operation involved a list of 7,200 UK individuals (predominately men) sent by the FBI to the British Criminal Justice Agency, who had used their credit cards to pay to download sexual pictures of children from a website based in Texas. The Americans on the list were arrested simultaneously. However, in the UK, the British police forces have been slowly going through the UK list and prosecuting a few at a time. This has led to a great deal of anxiety with people who either know or fear that they may be on the list. Many have rushed to counsellors and psychologists, either in a genuine need to unload or change, or to prepare their defence in advance. It is important to add that these people are not the stereotype of a computer geek but predominantly white middle-class to upper-class professionals: paediatricians, teachers, judges, lawyers and sometimes quite elderly.

The biggest problem with child porn on the Internet is that prosecutions are very difficult as each country has differing laws both about sex with children and with viewing it on screen. In some countries, like Japan, it is not an offence to have pictures of children in sexually provocative poses, providing the vaginal cleft is covered even by a blade of grass (Jenkins, 2001), or to carry child pornography. But in the UK under the Sexual Offences Act 2003 it is an offence to have an indecent photograph or pseudo-photo of a child in his or her possession. In parenthesis, this has created a real problem for psychologists in that research cannot be conducted into this area, as both in this country and in the US it is illegal to look at as well as to possess pictures. Some high-profile defences on the grounds of conducting research have been dismissed. Thus, in order for any enforcement policies to be effective, it requires some countries to change their thinking about the pictures that are currently available. In the UK it is considered that child pornography involves the physical, sexual and emotional abuse of a child, and viewing pictures of it subsequently perpetuates abuse.

Is there a close connection between looking and doing? Here again, paedophilia is not a unitary concept, and can be subdivided into infantile (nepiophilia), juvenile (paedophilia) and adolescent (ephebophilia). A large majority of paedophiles will be ephebophiliacs who enjoy viewing pictures of post-pubescent yet legally underage adolescents. In the Internet world, such material is called 'loli' (Lolita) sites. The vast majority of these people are what have been termed 'affectionate paedophiles' (Money, 1986) and would not dream of physically hurting a child. Unfortunately, the tabloid press has contributed to the blurring of these different forms of paraphilia to suggest that all paedophiles are also murderers of children. As Money (1986) points out, a lust murderer with erotophonophilia (Greek: *eros*: love + *phonein*: to murder) may have children as his victims, but these people are going to be a very small minority of those who are sexually aroused by children. Jenkins (2001) highlights this distinction in the group discussion among Internet 'pedos'. These are a distinct group of self-confessed paedophiles, who meet in social cyberspace. They have their own moralities and their own language. They are very clear that they look at children and enjoy the pictures, but they do not touch them. They believe that theirs is a true love of children and that looking does no harm. They also enjoy the process of collecting the pictures, which are not purely for masturbatory purposes but for collection's sake. They like the danger of what they do and enjoy the banter of challenging potential LEAs (law enforcement agencies) and frequently share 'safe surfing' strategies. They believe that all men are 'pedos' but that they are the only ones honest enough to admit it. Denial tends to be a big factor in their 'look don't touch' morality, however, as many had to provide photographs of children in order to gain access to child porn sites. Even if they did not have to do this, their activity can only feed off those who abuse children in this way.

To return to the client in the question, it may be helpful to specifically ask if the client is viewing and downloading pictures of children on the Internet, as it is vital to be fully cognizant of what is being presented. If he is, the counsellor has an ethical dilemma, as the client is committing a criminal offence, although there is no requirement within the Sexual Offences Act to inform the authorities of this information. The counsellor will need to consider whether the client's law-breaking justifies a breach of confidentiality. To reiterate, child pornography is considered by many to be a form of sexual abuse. Thus some argue that looking *is* doing. An alternative argument is that paedophilia is merely another form of sexual orientation (see Question 8.1), which is inherent in *Homo sapiens* and can be traced back to ancient civilizations. And, as I have indicated in other answers, there are many shades of grey in the continuum of sexual behaviour.

Recent guidelines produced by the Department of Health (DoH 2003) following the Laming Report into the death of Victoria Climbié insist on interagency sharing of any threats to children with sexual, emotional, or physical abuse, and emphasize the importance of interagency cooperation. Although legally a counsellor is under no obligation to disclose abusive practice, the DoH have made it clear that, if counsellors work in the NHS, the expectation will be to inform, and failure to do so would leave them open to severe criticism. This is also true of some other settings, such as social services or agencies funded by social services. This applies to physical, emotional or sexual abuse, or to a child living within a family in which domestic violence occurs. Yet someone has to help sexual offenders of all persuasions, and breaching confidentiality when they have asked for help might also be viewed as anti-therapeutic. Indeed, it could be argued that good therapy with such clients contributes to the protection of future children from abuse.

If the client in this question does want to change his behaviour, he will need specialist help. Many paedophiles have no wish to change. What they want is to continue with the behaviour they enjoy but want help to avoid the aversive consequences that go with it. Unfortunately, there is virtually no immediate help for sexual offenders except through the forensic system, which requires that the person has committed the offence first, and thus the help becomes a consequent requirement of the sentencing. Similarly, in the UK, there is no facility in the system for an astute therapist to identify a person who is about to embark on a criminal activity and to offer that person specialist therapeutic help to prevent it.

* * *

9.2 I am seeing a man who spends hours watching porn on the Internet. He is not in a relationship, so is this a problem for him? What sort of treatment is available for sexual addiction?

This question has four components to it: use of the Internet (as discussed in the answer to Question 9.1), the use of pornography, the concept of sexual addiction (which is controversial in the therapeutic literature) and, finally, treatment interventions.

What is pornography? The *Oxford Dictionary* of 1864 describes it as 'the life, manners, etc of prostitutes and their patrons'. This suggests that pictures of spouses having sexual intercourse are not pornographic. This reflects a classic male Victorian notion that such behaviour was not the sort of behaviour one undertook with one's wife. The Williams Committee on Obscenity and Film Censorship in 1979 later defined pornography as:

A pornographic representation is one that combines two features: it has a certain function or intention, to arouse its audience sexually, and also a certain content, explicit representations of sexual material (organs, postures, activity etc.). A work has to have both this function and this content to be a piece of pornography.

Fisher and Barak (2001) question how to define sexually explicit materials and break pornography down into three separate categories:

- erotica – sexually explicit non-degrading, non-violent portrayal of consensual sexual activity
- degrading pornography – sexually explicit that degrades, debases and dehumanizes people, usually women, but sometimes men
- violent pornography – material that endorses the utility and normativeness of sexual violence, usually directed by men against women.

The United States Senate tried to ban pornography on the Internet, to the wrath and eventual success of the civil libertarians, who got the laws revoked on the grounds that the law was unconstitutional in invading people's basic freedom to express their own sexuality. They idealized the porn myth that porn frees the libido and gives men an outlet for sexual expression. However, rather than liberate men, porn can be a source of bondage as they search the Net, craving for the 'right' image for masturbatory relief. The more time they spend in their fantasy world, the more difficult it is to make the transition back to reality. One therapist wrote: 'In over 26 years, I have treated approximately 350 males afflicted with sexual addictions. In about 94% of cases I have found pornography was a contributor, facilitator, or direct causal agent in acquiring this sexual illness' (Cline, 1996: 58).

The controversy over whether sexual addiction actually exists is currently being argued in the literature. Some maintain that it is a form of hypersexuality (as discussed in the answer to Question 6.3). Others have argued for it being a manifestation of sexual compulsivity or sexual impulsivity. Sexual compulsivity, Coleman (1990) argues, is very similar to obsessive-compulsive disorder (OCD), but here the anxiety-driven behaviour manifests itself in sexual activity. It involves intrusive, uncontrollable thoughts, rigidly repetitive behaviours to reduce distress and meaningless maladaptive behavioural patterns. It is distressing, obstructive and unpleasant. Quadland (1985) defines sexual compulsiveness as 'a compelling activity from which the person derives no pleasure'. He emphasizes a lack of control over sexual behaviour, low sexual satisfaction and a dissociation between love, affection and sexual behaviour. In addition, the individual experiences high anxiety levels, in which the excessive sexual behaviour detracts from the anxiety – once again similar to OCD. However, Cooper's (1998) large Internet survey discussed in the answer to Question 9.1 scored respondents on a sexual-compulsivity scale and found that frequent cyber-sex behaviour was not synonymous with sexual compulsion.

Sexual impulsivity, described by Barth and Kinder (1987) as an atypical impulse control disorder, consists of a failure to resist an impulse, drive or temptation that is harmful to oneself or another. It may or may not be conscious resistance and may or may not be premeditated or planned. It involves increased tension before the behaviour and pleasure or gratification or release at the time of the behaviour. The individual may or may not feel regret, self-reproach or guilt after the behaviour. It appears that the only difference between the concepts of sexual compulsivity and sexual impulsivity is whether or not the person feels pleasure (and therefore is sexually satisfied) when undertaking the activity: if they enjoy masturbating on the Internet, it is impulsive; if they do not, it is compulsive.

What is sexual addiction? Can this be a reason why people spend so long involved in cybersex? The diagnostic criteria for sexual addiction proposed by Goodman (1992) are:

- recurrent failure to resist impulses to engage in a specified sexual behaviour
- increased sense of tension immediately prior to initiating the sexual behaviour
- pleasure or relief at the time of engaging in sexual behaviour
- symptoms persisting for more than one month
- at least five of the following:

  - frequent preoccupation in preparation for sex
  - frequent engagement in the sexual activity or extending over a long period
  - repeated efforts to reduce, control or stop the sexual behaviour
  - a great deal of time spent on it or recovering from it
  - being sexual when the person should be doing other things (like working)
  - giving up other activities to make time for sex
  - continuing despite negative consequences
  - tolerance – need to increase the intensity to get the same thrill
  - restlessness or irritability if not engaging

Of course, there have been criticisms of this definition, such as Mosner (1992), who argues that honeymooners might also fit into these criteria!

Carnes et al. (2001) describe the levels of addictive sexual behaviours and how these can be played out via the Internet. They view addictive behaviour as progressing through three hierarchical levels. Repetitive sexual behaviour is intense and invokes the sympathetic nervous system, producing an adrenaline surge to provide physiological addiction as well as psychological dependency. They argue that, as people become more desen-sitized to their own sexual behaviour, they need greater levels of stimulation to get the same thrill. Thus tolerance and escalation, the same as any other addiction to an external substance like drugs or alcohol, appear to become common factors. The three levels are:

- Level 1: These behaviours are generally socially accepted so have public tolerance even though they are regarded as unseemly or even illegal:
  - compulsive masturbation
  - multiple simultaneous relationships
  - 800/900 dial-up telephone sex
  - sexual chat rooms
  - browsing visual stimulation: centrefolds, paper, video and internet pornography, strip shows, sex shops
  - using prostitutes/sex workers
  - anonymous sex, one-night stands

Level 1 addicts move from passing interest into obsession. They ration-alize their behaviour as being acceptable, for example just being a full-blooded male or not hurting anyone else. They deny the consequences in terms of money, time, control, personal pain and loneliness. They fre-quently promise to give up when the time is right and progressively retreat from the reality of family, friends and work into their secret double life, the real world and the addicted world.

- Level 2: This usually involves behaviours with legal sanctions:
  - exhibitionism – first as covert flashers, then moving on to announc-ing sexual behaviour and inviting strangers to watch: 'dogging'
  - voyeurism
  - offensive phone calls
  - illicit frottage – rubbing against people in crowded places
  - exhibitionist-voyeuristic combined – e.g. watching and masturbating via Internet web cameras: called 'cuseeme' technology

- Level 3: All boundaries of society are swept away as the addict moves into needing to maintain the highest levels of sexual excitation and ful-filment.
  - rape
  - incest
  - child molestation
  - bestiality
  - sadomasochism

Carnes et al. (2001) point out that rape is the most extreme expression of sexual addiction; although not all rapists are addicts, some addicts are rapists. And not all sex addicts become sex offenders; only 55% of sex offenders are sex addicts. However, deviancy does involve risk, and risk seems to be sufficiently mood-altering to invoke addictive processes central to the process of escalation. They also point out the correlation between sexual addiction and other forms of addictive behaviour: drinking, drugs, overeating, overworking and gambling. They are mutually irresistible and intoxicating.

Some of the elements of Internet addiction involve learning new experiences and a sexual repertoire previously not encountered, for example golden rain (urination during a sexual encounter), fisting (pushing the fist through anus or vagina), rimming (licking anus and perineum) etc. It also involves relationship regression; the more time is spent on the Net, the less time there is for real intimacy and real relationships. Cybersex can also lead to other inappropriate behaviours, like stealing or embezzling money to pay for the costs of club memberships. It may be a catalyst and precipitate real off-line sexual behaviour as desensitization and tolerance occurs. And the computer and Internet per se may become a fetish and create arousal at the touch of a keyboard or the click of a mouse. Schneider (2000) highlights the adverse consequences of cybersex addiction, including depression, social isolation, relationship problems, inadvertent exposure of children to online pornography, decreased job performance or job loss, financial debts and cyberstalking. Denial is a contributory factor in cybersex, with rationalizations such as:

• Because it is virtual, it is not real.
• This is only sexual fantasy, which is normal.
• I'm not really being unfaithful.
• No one is being hurt.
• I can stop whenever I want.
• I'll just do it for another half hour.

Schneider (1994) emphasizes that, in order to assess cybersex addiction, you need to consider three criteria:

1. The loss of freedom or will to engage in behaviour or not; the compulsivity of the behaviour
2. The continuation of behaviour despite adverse consequences, usually in terms of family, financial or occupational prohibition
3. Obsession with the behaviour, as it moves from a passing interest into an obsession

If it is accepted that not all cybersex is negative, how can counsellors determine if it is problematic when denial plays such a big part in the process? Some key questions to ask are:

- Do you do this to alter your mood?
- Does this interfere with your daily living – work, home, family?
- Is it being used for arousal and orgasm, rather than just arousal for real sexual activity?
- Is the Internet taking you away from real sexual relationships rather than enhancing them?

Another indication for the counsellor is whether the addictive cycle can be identified (Carnes et al., 2001). This behavioural pattern involves a pre-occupation with the thoughts about the behaviour, moving into ritualization in preparation for undertaking the behaviour, conducting the behaviour, then feeling bad – shame or disgust – about the behaviour and back to intrusive thoughts making the preoccupation occur again (see Figure 9.1).

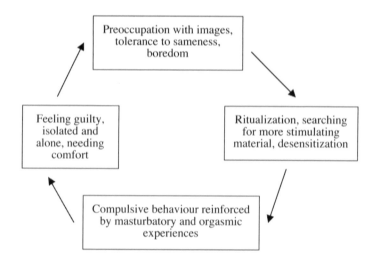

Figure 9.1 The cycle of addiction, after Carnes et al., (2001).

Treatment approaches for sexual addiction tend to revolve around the therapist's view of what underpins the behaviour. The addictions model uses the Alcoholics Anonymous (AA) twelve-step approach to addiction (Carnes et al., 2001). Also advocated are group psychotherapy, pharmacology (for those that follow the compulsivity/hypersexuality view), individual psychotherapy, Cognitive Behaviour Therapy (CBT) and Internet-based email therapy (although this must be like using whiskey to make an alcoholic better!).

The value of medication should not be overlooked for some clients who feel they need ongoing support through counselling therapy. SSRIs (Specific Serotonin Reuptake Inhibitors) like fluoxetine (Prozac), sertraline (Zoloft), paroxetine (Seroxat), citalopram (Celexa) and the mood stabilizer lithium carbonate can be prescribed to reduce or eliminate sexual desire and obsessive-compulsive symptoms. We do not know if the successful results are due to the client's elevated mood or the inhibition of his or her sexual desire from the inevitable side effects of the drugs. In addition to the medication, CBT may be helpful in changing core beliefs, managing stress, enhancing relationships and social and communication skills, and readjusting to healthy sexual practices.

Carnes et al. (2001) argue that by using the twelve-step programme of AA, an addict can move into recovery by changing his or her faulty core beliefs. They advocate the twelve steps as the means by which an addict can develop meaningful relationships. The person has to admit powerlessness over the addiction, and, by giving themselves over to a higher power, they will be restored to sanity, and as such develop new core beliefs. They also provide additional support using peers and spiritual pathways. Time-limited abstinence or celibacy contracts are advocated using the SAFE model as a formula of sexual activity. As sexual behaviour is a biological need, going cold turkey may not always be the best option. So the SAFE formula was developed to help addicts determine if their sexual behaviour was appropriate. If the sex is:

- **S**ecret – behaviour that would not be acceptable to public scrutiny
- **A**busive – exploitative or harmful to self or others
- **F**eelings – sex is used to alter or remove painful moods
- **E**mpty – of caring or fulfilling relationships, then it is not safe.

Whatever a counsellor's theoretical orientation, he or she can undertake some useful therapeutic work by using the treatment proposals of Delmonico et al., (2002). They have adapted the concepts of first-order and second-order changes into a pragmatic therapeutic strategy for those addicted to the Internet. The first-order changes are concrete actions to quickly stop an escalating problem that is likely to lead to negative consequences. It is the crisis treatment of cybersex. The second-order changes are actions taken to produce long-term effects at a deeper therapeutic level.

- First-order changes:
    - *Reducing access to the computer*: changing its location, letting others see the screen, self-limiting surfing time with no cybersex activity, using inbuilt Internet filters etc.
    - *Confront the myth of anonymity*: the concept that no one knows what is happening is a myth. The history of Internet usage is compiled on the

hard drive, and different Internet sites download cookies onto the system that spy on the user to view where the person surfs. This allows for appropriate spam advertising to be sent in accordance with their surfing activities. Software can be downloaded to identify the surveillance products already on their PC.

- *Raising awareness*: providing tasks that help break through clients' denial, like making lists of consequences, discussing the effects on others, perhaps involving significant others to break through his or her denial.
- *Identifying triggers*: identifying triggers that precipitate unwanted behaviour.
- *Identifying motivation*: some people stop the behaviour because of external pressures (partner, boss). When these pressures have been resolved, relapse potential is high until the client moves from external to internal motivation.

• Second-order changes:

- *Attacking the cycle*: finding the appropriate place to break the cycle of addiction and reduce the intensity of the addiction.
- *Co-morbid issues*: check out for depression, anxiety or OCD rituals, unresolved grief, childhood trauma and develop new ways of dealing with stress.
- *Conduct therapy with partner* or family to reduce collateral damage. Encourage movement away from isolated Internet activities to real communication with real people and healthy sexual activity.
- *Develop a support network* of friends and supporters to help through the times of difficulty.
- *Relapse prevention*: preparing strategies when temptation is very strong.

***

9.3 What makes a person develop unusual or bizarre sexual practices? Does anything go these days? I sometimes feel rather uncomfortable when I hear some of the things clients get up to.

Unusual or bizarre sexual practices are called paraphilias (Greek – *para*: unusual, *philia*: love). There is a vast range of paraphilias that individuals may acquire. Money (1986) divides them up into six categories:

• *Sacrificial and expiatory*: requires sinful lust and consequent atonement in the behaviour. Sadism, masochism, and lustful murder fit in this category, as do coprophilia (love of excreta) and urophilia (love of urine, 'golden rain').

- *Marauding and predatory*: taking love by stealth without consent or force. Rape, kleptophilia (stealing sexual objects) and necrophilia (sex with a corpse).
- *Mercantile and venal*: sex that is bartered, traded or paid for. Prostitution, live sex shows, telephone sex (telephonicophilia).
- *Fetishistic and talisman*: token, fetish or talisman substitutes for the lover. Touch of fabrics like rubber or leather (hyphephilia) or smells (olfactophilia), the touch of insects or animals in the genital areas (formicophilia) or the feel of enemas in the anal passages (klismophilia). Transvestitism also falls into this category.
- *Stigmatic and eligibilic*: the partner must be stigmatised, ostracised as an outsider, or physically handicapped, like amputees (acrotomophilia). Paedophilia and gerontophilia (sex with an elder person) also fit into this category, as does zoophilia (sex with animals).
- *Solicitational and allurative*: displaying, watching, touching, rubbing, etc. to elicit a sexual encounter. Exhibitionism (peodeiktophilia – flashing), voyeurism (scoptophilia – peeping Tom), providing live sex shows (autoagonistophilia), frottage (illicit rubbing – very common on the London Underground!), promiscuity and pornography fall into this category, as does stigmatophilia: being pierced, mutilated or tattooed is also considered allurative.

Money (1986) believes that paraphilias are not generated at random but fall into the categories above due to a vandalized and redesigned lovemap caused by the neglect, traumatization or suppression of the normal heterosexual lovemap development. This vandalism creates distortions, displacements, omissions or inclusions in the individual's sexual repertoire, and become the only channel through which sexual arousal and climax can take place. This lovemap pathology manifests in full after puberty and is not subject to voluntary control. Each paraphilia has a dual existence: one in fantasy, and one where the fantasy is played out in practice. It has also been noticed that many clients who demonstrate paraphilias have more than one, suggesting there may be a biological basis for them. Money believes that it is essentially a developmental disability and that boys are more predisposed to the development of a paraphilia than girls. He argues that it is wrong to call them sexual disorders, as they are really a disorder of pair-bonding or attachment. Thus they are a disorder of love not lust.

It can be difficult for a counsellor to hear about the unusual sexual practices that form a normal part of some clients' sexual repertoire. It may be that the client has not told anyone else other than the counsellor of the behaviour; so it is vital that the counsellor remains neutral in receiving the information. If unsure what the activity involves, asking for more information can help formulate hypotheses as to what may underpin it. Using an attachment frame, the counsellor may help the client replace unusual practices with behaviours that make them feel more secure. As with other psychological disorders, the best treatment outcome, with less likelihood of relapse, are those that use pharmacology and talking therapies combined.

* * *

9.4 I have been working with a young man who steals women's knickers from stores, or even from female friends' rooms. He can't help himself, but fears getting caught. Is this a fetish? And how might I understand what is going on in him?

Kleptophilia (Greek – *kletein*: to steal, *philia*: love) is a paraphilia of the marauding/predatory type (see Question 9.3) and is the erotic version of kleptomania, the obsessive desire to steal. The objects stolen are often valueless, as the desire is the stealing per se not the ownership of the object obtained. Thus a man who compulsively steals women's knickers is showing kleptophilia. If the act of stealing produces an orgasm or ejaculation, this is called kleptolangia, and is thought to be due to an internalized sexual psychopathology (Eskapa, 1995). The fetishistic side of this behaviour is if the person is doing so for autoerotic reasons. It may be the sight, touch or smell of the stolen knickers that only allows him to become aroused and achieve an orgasm. Some men will like to wear them; others will put them on their heads, over their faces or tuck them into their own underwear.

Goldman (1991) suggests that the need to steal valueless objects comes from dysphoric individuals (often women) who have sexual difficulties and a history of a tumultuous and stressful childhood. The act of stealing will provide heightened arousal, similar to sexual activity. Therefore stealing a sexual object may increase this arousal level even higher. It is likely that the fetishistic behaviour towards the underwear occurred first, and the desire to steal them came later as the fetish became desensitized. Such fetishes are also insatiable; it would be insufficient to have one pair of knickers, one would need a veritable collection of them.

A fetish is a conditioned or learned response, usually established during a critical period during the individual's sexual development. As such, it needs to be deconditioned and replaced by more appropriate behaviour. If the counsellor has a psychodynamic orientation, some useful work can focus on the origins of the fetish, often developed during puberty or adolescence. Often the client will experience deep feelings of guilt and shame, and helping work through those will reduce the cyclical need to do it (see the addictive cycle in Question 9.2). If the counsellor uses a cognitive orientation, homework on desensitizing the erotic behaviour and replacing it with a different stimulus can be helpful. Kafka (2001) also proposes pharmacological interventions alongside therapy to enhance the struggle for self-control. Counsellors need to consider that although kleptophilia may sound rather innocuous, if the client is stealing from people rather than from shops, he is doing so because he is fantasizing about a relationship with that person, and thus is doing so without consent. When tolerance occurs to that behaviour, it can lead to other forms of sexual behaviour involving taking sexual favours without consent, which can escalate to groping, sexual assault or rape.

* * *

9.5 Why do some people get turned on by pain? One of my clients regularly visits an S and M club but seems to see nothing odd about it. I am concerned about him: is it me who has the problem or him?

Sex throughout history has always had a close association with aggression, thought to be due to the archaic reptilian complex still embedded in the brain stem. As sex is associated with aggression, it is, as a consequence, also associated with pain. Indeed, there are many who would argue that rape is not about sex at all but about power, domination and humiliation. Thus a close connection is inevitable between sex and those who get turned on by inflicting pain. Sadism came to be named after the Marquis de Sade, a French writer of the eighteenth century who described the phenomenon. Meloy (1992) describes sexual sadism as:

> The conscious experience of pleasurable sexual arousal through the infliction of physical or emotional pain on the actual object. (Meloy, 1992: 76)

Similarly, there are those who get turned on by receiving pain, being shamed, humiliated or dominated, termed masochism. Such behaviour is thought to be underpinned by severe childhood punishment that has become eroticized.

An ideal dynamic might therefore be a sadomasochistic couple, where one partner enjoys giving the pain and humiliation that the other enjoys receiving. Such practices might range from the mild infliction of pain, for example the man who enjoys his wife putting him in nappies and spanking his bare bottom, to the other end of the spectrum where one partner likes bondage: to be severely tied, handcuffed, beaten or having electrodes attached to his testicles. These couples often share a safeword, or password, between them that they can use when they feel that the pain threshold has been reached, which stops the couple from going too far. They may also engage in counting games, which are like rituals of whipping, flogging or spanking during which the submissive is required to keep count of the strokes delivered, to thank the dominant for each one and then ask for more.

But why do some people enjoy the pain aspect, where as for others any sort of pain of discomfort is a complete turn off? Money (1986), as discussed in the answer to Question 9.3, suggests that it is because the lovemap of a person's sexuality, which developed at between five and eight years old, has been vandalized by actual or vicarious abusive practices. Tiger (1992) agrees that children who are beaten by their parents learn to associate love with pain as they vie for attention. Even negative punishment to a child is more rewarding than no attention at all. Margolis (2004) highlights the blurring between sex and aggression by pointing out that some boxers get so turned on in the boxing ring that they ejaculate. Others suggest that these paraphilias are developed as a result of temporal lobe damage or epilepsy, which may occur during infancy.

If the client in this question has no problem with his sexuality, and he is only engaged in sexual activity with consenting adults, the counsellor need not be focused on trying to resolve the behaviour unless asked to do so by the client. However, the client may present with 'Monday morning rebound syndrome', which is when feelings of fear, disgust, self-loathing or remorse emerge hours or days after engaging in S and M activities, in which case the client may ask for help in stopping. Sadists also might present with difficulties of hyposexuality, retarded ejaculation or erectile failure. Similarly, masochists may present with premature ejaculation and loss of libido as the behaviour becomes desensitised. Cognitive Behaviour Therapy and psychodynamic therapies are equally valuable with these problems, especially when helped through pharmacology to reduce the hypersexual behaviour and compulsive thoughts, although the long-term prognosis for complete recovery is thought to be poor.

As an addendum to the concept of sexual sadism, the counsellor must be alert to whether the behaviour presented is associated with an antisocial personality disorder. Lunde and Morgan (1980) contend that there is a temporal coupling of erotic stimulation and violence in the childhood histories of all sexually psychopathic serial murderers (Gerberth, 1995). Therefore, for personal safety and the safety of others, a forensic referral in these cases might be thought to be essential.

Glossary

Androgens: steroids produced as hormones by the testes that promote male sexual organs and male secondary characteristics.

Androgynous: neither male nor female but a blend of both.

Chromosomes: each individual has a pair of sex chromosomes that helps determine their biological sex. Females have two X chromosomes, whereas males have one X and one Y.

Clitoridectomy: surgical removal of the clitoris.

Clitoromegaly: abnormally large clitoris.

Cross-dressers: people who enjoy wearing the clothing of the 'opposite' biological sex.

Cybersex: a sexual interaction between at least two persons via the Internet.

Erotic transference: a healthy love relationship between therapist and client that forms part of the therapeutic alliance and work.

Eroticized transference: a severe, tenacious, and a delusional disturbance of attachment of the client to the therapist.

Fistula: an abnormal opening on the skin between two internal organs.

Gender dysphoria (Gender Identity Disorder): a strong and persistent cross-gender identification, and a persistent discomfort and distress with his or her own biological sex.

Gonads: ovaries in women and testes in men.

Homophobia: a morbid dislike of homosexuals.

Hymen: a fold of skin in the outer portion of the vaginal barrel that occludes the passage and tears with penetrative sex.

Hypospadia: a congenital malformation of the urethral canal.

Hysterectomy: surgical removal of the uterus.

Iatrogenic: induced in a patient as a result of a physician's actions.

Infibulation: to close female genitalia with stitches or clips to prevent sexual intercourse.

Intersex: a person born with both male and female or ambiguous genitalia.

Isosexuality: sex performed by animals with others of the same biological sex.

Karyotype: the appearance of specific chromosomes in a cell.

Masochism: sexual pleasure derived from pain or humiliation.

Mastectomy: surgical removal of the breast.

Menopause: the ending of a woman's menstrual cycle.

Oophorectomy: surgical removal of the ovary.

Orchidectomy: surgical removal of the testicle.

Paraphilia: unusual or deviant sexual practice.

Phalloplasty: surgical construction of the penis.

Priapism: an unduly long and painful erection.

Prostatectomy: surgical removal of the prostate gland.

Psychogenic: symptoms of psychological rather than organic causation.

Sadism: sexual pleasure derived from the infliction of pain or mental suffering on another.

Scrotoplasty: surgical construction of the scrotum.

Stenosis: the narrowing of the bowel or rectum.

Sterilization: the closing of the Fallopian tubes as a means of contraception.

Thrombo-embolic: obstruction of a blood vessel by a blood clot.

Transgenderist (Trans): a person who breaks away from society's expectations of female or male in their gender identity, gender presentation or gender experiences.

Transsexuals: a person who has demonstrated at least two years of wanting, or who actually has had, a surgical reassignment to the opposite biological sex.

Vaginoplasty: surgical construction of the vagina.

Vasectomy: a minor surgical procedure that cuts the vas deferens, the tubes that deliver the sperm from the testes in a man, a method of contraception.

Virilization: to be made manly or to develop male characteristics.

Useful addresses

APN: Association of Psychosexual Nursing
PO Box 2762
London W1A 5HQ
www.wanstead.park.btinternet.co.uk

BASRT: British Association for Sexual and Relationship Therapy
PO Box 13686
London SW20 9ZH
Tel: 020 8543 2707
www.basrt.org.uk

The Beaumont Society
27 Old Gloucester Street
London WC1N 3XX
Tel: 01582 412 220
www.beaumontsociety.org.uk

Couple Counselling Scotland
18 York Place
Edinburgh EH1 3EP
Tel: 0131 558 9669
www.couplecounselling.org

The Gender Trust
PO Box 3192
Brighton BN1 3WR
Tel: 0700 790 347
www.gendertrust.org.uk

IPM: Institute of Psychosexual Medicine
12 Chandos Street
Cavendish Square
London W1G 9DR
Tel: 020 7580 0631
www.ipm.org.uk

PTS: Pink Therapy Services
BCM Box 5159
London WC1N 3XX
Tel: 020 7291 4480
www.pinktherapy.com

Relate
Herbert Gray College
Little Church Street
Rugby
Warwickshire CV21 3AP
Tel: 01788 573241
www.relate.org.uk

Sexual Dysfunction Association
Windmill Place Business Centre
2-4 Windmill Lane
Southall
Middlesex UB2 4NJ
Tel: 0870 774 3571
www.sda.uk.net

UKIA: The UK Intersex Association
www.ukia.co.uk

References

Ahmed A (1997) Peyronie's disease. British Journal of Sexual Medicine 24(6): 22–23.

Ainsworth MDS (1979) Attachment as related to mother–infant interaction. Advances in the Study of Behaviour 9: 2–52.

Akdeniz Y (1999) Sex on the Net. Reading: South Street Press.

Annon JS (1976) The PLISSIT model: a proposed conceptual scheme for the behavioural treatment of sexual problems. Journal of Sexual Education & Therapy 2(2): 1–15.

Apfelbaum B (1983) Expanding the Boundaries of Sex Therapy: The Ego-Analytical Model. Berkeley CA: Berkeley Sex Therapy Group.

Ayles MD, Reynolds J (2001) Identifying and managing patients' relationship problems in primary care: the perspective of health professionals and counsellors. London: One Plus One.

Bancroft J (1989) Human Sexuality and its Problems (2nd edn.) New York: Churchill Livingstone.

Bancroft J, Janssen E, Strong D et al. (2003a) The relation between mood and sexuality in heterosexual men. Archives of Sexual Behaviour, 32(3): 217–230.

Bancroft J, Janssen E, Strong D et al. (2003b) The relation between mood and sexuality in gay men. Archives of Sexual Behaviour 32(3): 231–242.

Bancroft J, Vukadinovic Z (2004) Sexual addiction, sexual compulsivity, sexual impulsivity, or what? Journal of Sex Research 41(3): 225–234.

Barth RJ, Kinder BN (1987) The mislabelling of sexual impulsivity. Journal of Sex & Marital Therapy 13(1): 12–13.

Bass E, Davies L (1988) The Courage to Heal. A Guide for Women Survivors of Sexual Abuse. New York: Harpers & Row.

Baumeister RF (2004) Gender and erotic plasticity: sociocultural influences on the sex drive. Sexual and Marital Therapy 19(2): 133–139.

Beck AT (1988) Love is Never Enough. New York: Penguin.

Bem DJ (1996) Exotic becomes erotic: A developmental theory of sexual orientation. Psychological Review 103(2): 320–335.

Bem SL (1975) Sex role adaptability: one consequence of psychological androgyny. Journal of Personality & Social Psychology 31(4): 634–643.

Benjamin H (1966) The Transsexual Phenomenon. New York: The Julian Press.

Bing E, Coleman L (1977) Making Love During Pregnancy. New York: Noonday Press.

Blanchard R, Steiner BW, Clemmensen LH (1985) Gender dysphoria, gender reorientation and the clinical management of transsexuals. Journal of Consultant Clinical Psychology 53: 295–304.

Blum HP (1973) The concept of erotized transference. Journal of American Psychoanalytic Association 21(1): 61–76.

Bowlby J (1951) Child Care and the Growth of Love. Harmondsworth: Penguin.

Brindley GS (1996) Intrapenile drug delivery systems. International Journal of STD & AIDS 7(suppl. 3): 13–15.

Burke Drauker C (1992) Counselling Survivors of Childhood Sexual Abuse. London: Sage.

Carnes P, Delmonico DL, Griffin E (2001) In the Shadows of the Net. Breaking Free of Compulsive Online Sexual Behaviour. Minnesota: Hazelden.

Clarkson P (2003) No sex please, we're counsellors. Counselling & Psychotherapy Journal 14(2): 7–10.

Cline VB (1996) Pornography and sexual addictions. Christian Counselling Today 4(4): 58.

Coleman E (1990) The obsessive–compulsive model for describing compulsive sexual behaviour. American Journal of Preventive Psychiatry and Neurology 1: 9–14.

Cooper A (1998) Sexuality and the Internet: Surfing into the next millennium. CyberPsychology & Behaviour 1(2): 187–193.

Cooper A, Boies S, Maheu M et al. (1999) Sexuality and the Internet: The next sexual revolution. In Muscarella F, Szuchman L (eds.), The Psychological Science of Sexuality: A Research Based Approach. New York: Wiley.

Costa P, Jaccovella J, Bouvet A (1997) Efficacy and tolerability of moxisylyte and placebo injected intracavernosally in patients with erectile dysfunction (ED): a multi-centre double-blind study. Paper presented at the British Erectile Disorder Society Annual Conference, Stratford on Avon.

Croft LH (1982) Sexuality in the Later Years. Boston: John Wright.

Crowe M, Ridley J (1986) The negotiated timetable: a new approach to marital conflicts involving male demands and female reluctance for sex. Sexual and Marital Therapy 1(2): 157–173.

Crowe M, Ridley J (1990) Therapy with Couples. A Behavioural-Systems Approach to Marital and Sexual Problems. Oxford: Blackwell Science.

Daines B, Perrett A (2000) Psychodynamic Approaches to Sexual Problems. Buckingham: Open University Press.

de Waal FBM (1995) Sex as an alternative to aggression in the bonobo. In Abramson PR, Pinkerton SD (eds.), Sexual Nature Sexual Culture. London: University of Chicago Press.

Delmonico DL, Griffin E, Carnes P (2002) Treating online compulsive sexual behaviour: When cybersex is the drug of choice. In Cooper A (ed.), Sex and the Internet. A Guidebook for Clinicians. New York: Brunner-Routledge.

Diamond MA (1979) Sexual identity and sex roles. In Bullough VL (ed.), The Frontiers of Sex Research. New York: Prometheus.

DoH (2003) Co-Operating to Safeguard Children. London: HMSO.

DSM-IV (1994) Diagnostic and Statistical Manual of Mental Disorders. Washington DC: American Psychiatric Association.

Duck S (1986) Human Relationships. An Introduction to Social Psychology. London: Sage.

Eardley I (2004) Sex and the Prostate. Paper presented at the European Federation of Sexology Congress 2004, Brighton.

Eastham JA, Riedel E, Scardino PT et al. (2003) Variation of serum prostate-specific antigen levels. An evaluation of year-to-year fluctuations. Journal of American Medical Association 289(20): 2695–2700.

Elkins R (1997) Male Femaling: A Grounded Theory Approach to Cross-Dressing and Sex-Changing. London: Routledge.

Eskapa R (1995) Bizarre Sex. Avonmouth: Parallel Books.

Fallowfield L (2004) Setting the scene: the problem of cancer and sexuality. Paper presented at the European Federation of Sexology Congress 2004, Brighton.

Farley F (1986) The world of the type-T personality. Psychology Today (May): 45–52.

Fausto-Sterling A (1944, 1992) Myths of Gender (2nd edn.) New York: Basic Books.

Feldman HA, Goldstein I, Hatzichristou DG et al. (1994) Impotence and its medical and psychosocial correlates: Results of the Massachusetts male aging study. Journal of Urology 151(1): 54–61.

Field N (1996) Breakdown and Breakthrough. Psychotherapy in a New Dimension. London: Routledge.

Finkelhor D (1984) Child Sexual Abuse: New Theory and Research. New York: Free Press.

Fisher WA, Barak A (2001) Internet pornography: a social psychological perspective on internet sexuality. Journal of Sex Research 38: 312–323.

Fiske S, Taylor SE (1991) Social Cognition. New York: McGraw-Hill.

Fonaghy P (2001) Attachment Theory and Psychoanalysis. New York: Other Press.

Forbes A (2004) It's all back to front. Positive Nation (Dec–Jan 2003/2004): 36–38.

Freud S (1901) The Psychopathology of Everyday Life. The Standard Edition of the Complete Works of Sigmund Freud (Vol. 6), (trans. Strachey J). London: Hogarth.

Freud S (1915) Observations on transference-love: further recommendations on the technique of psycho-analysis, III, The Standard Edition of the Complete Psychological Works of Sigmund Freud (Vol. 12), (trans. Strachey J). London: Hogarth Press.

Gabbard G (1996) Love and Hate in an Analytic Setting. Northvale, NJ: Aronson.

Ganem M (2004) Pregnancy and Sexuality. Paper presented at the European Federation of Sexology Congress 2004, Brighton.

Garde I, Lunde I (1980) Female sexual behaviour. A study in a random sample of 40-year-old women. Maturitas 2: 240–255.

Gerberth VJ (1995) Psychopathic sexual sadists. The psychology and psychodynamics of serial killers. Law and Order 43(4): 4.

Gibson HB (1992) The Emotional and Sexual Lives of Older People. London: Chapman & Hall.

Gilman SE, Cochran SD, Mays VE et al. (2001) Risk of psychiatric disorders among individuals reporting same-sex sexual partners in the National Comorbidity Survey. American Journal of Public Health 91(6): 933–939.

Glanville M (1997) Natural Alternatives to HRT. London: Kyle Cathie.

Glanville M (2001) The Nutritional Health Handbook for Women. London: Judy Piatkus.

Glover J, Wylie K (1999) The importance of gender of the therapist to the patient presenting with sexual problems. Sexual and Marital Therapy 14(2): 137–142.

Goldman MJ (1991) Kleptomania: Making sense of the nonsensical. American Journal of Psychiatry 148(8): 986–996.

Goldmeir D (2001) 'Responsive' sexual desire in women – managing the normal? Sexual and Relationship Therapy 16(4): 381–388.

Golombok S, Spencer A, Rutter M (1983) Children in lesbian and single-parent households: psychosexual and psychiatric appraisal. Journal of Child Psychology and Psychiatry 24(4): 551–572.

Goodman A (1992) Diagnosis and treatment of sexual addiction. Journal of Sex & Marital Therapy 18(4): 303–314.

Gräfenberg E (1950) The role of the urethra in female orgasm. International Journal of Sexology 111(3): 145–148.

Griggs C (1998) S/He: Changing Sex and Changing Clothes. Oxford: Berg.

Groth AN (1979) Sexual trauma in the lives of rapists and child molesters. Victimology: An International Journal 4: 10–16.

Gundlach RH (1977) Sexual molestation and rape reported by homosexual and heterosexual women. Journal of Homosexuality 2(4): 367–384.

Hall J (1999) An exploration of the sexual and relationship experiences of lesbian survivors of childhood sexual abuse. Sexual and Marital Therapy 14(1): 61–70.

Harlow H (1971) Learning to Love. A Landmark Summary of Research Findings. New York: Ballantine Books.

Hasson HM (1993) Cervical removal at hysterectomy for benign disease. Risks and benefits. Journal of Reproductive Medicine 38(10): 781–790.

Hendrick C, Hendrick S, Foote F et al. (1984) Do men and women love differently? Journal of Social & Personal Relationships 1: 75–98.

Herdt G (1990) Developmental discontinuities and sexual orientation across cultures. In McWhirter DP, Sanders S, Reinisch JM (eds.), Homosexuality/Heterosexuality: Concepts of Sexual Orientation. New York: Oxford University Press.

Herman JL (1981) Father–Daughter Incest. Cambridge, MA: Harvard University.

Hillier J (2004) Feelings, sex and neurochemistry. Paper presented at the European Federation of Sexology Congress 2004, Brighton.

Hite S (1976) The Hite Report. New York: Macmillan.

Holmes S, Kirby R, Carson C (1997) Male Erectile Dysfunction. Oxford: Health Press.

House R (1996) Love, intimacy and therapeutic change. Self & Society 24(1): 21–26.

Howitt D (1995) Paedophiles and Sexual Offences Against Children. Chichester: Wiley.

Hudson-Allez G (1994) Contact in the Community: A Social Psychophysiological Approach. Bristol: University of Bristol.

Hudson-Allez G (1998) The interface between psychogenic and organic difficulties in men with erectile dysfunction. Sexual and Marital Therapy 13(3): 285–294.

Hudson-Allez G (2002) The prevalence of stalking of psychological therapists working in primary care by current or former clients. Counselling and Psychotherapy Research 2(2): 139–146.

Hudson-Allez G, Robertson N (2003) Medication. Prescribing for Emotional Distress and the use of Recreational Drugs. Bognor Regis: Association of Counsellors and Psychotherapists in Primary Care.

Istar Lev A (2004) Transgender Emergence. Therapeutic Guidelines for Working with Gender-variant People and their Families. New York: Haworth Press.

James A, Wilson K (1986) Couples, Conflict and Change. London: Tavistock.

Jayaratne TB (2002) White and African-American Genetic explanations for gender, class and race differences: The psychology of genetic beliefs. Invited lecture at the 2002 Human Genome lecture series, National Human Genome Research Institute, NIH. Bethesda, MD (June).

Jehu D (1988) Beyond Sexual Abuse. Chichester: Wiley.

Jenkins P (2001) Beyond Tolerance. Child Pornography on the Internet. New York: New York University Press.

Kafka MP (1997) Hypersexual desire in males: An operational definition and clinical implications for males with paraphilias and paraphilia-related disorders. Archives of Sexual Behaviour 26(5): 505–526.

Kafka MP (2001) The role of medications in the treatment of paraphilia-related disorders. Sexual and Relationship Therapy 16(6): 105–112.

Kalichman SC, Kelly JA, Morgan M et al. (1997) Fatalism, current life satisfaction, and risk for HIV infection among gay and bisexual men. Journal of Consulting & Clinical Psychology 65(4): 542–546.

Kaplan HS (1995) The Sexual Desire Disorders. New York: Bruner/Mazel.

Kephart WM (1967) Some correlates of romantic love. Journal of Marriage & the Family 29: 470–474.

Kinsey AC, Pomeroy WB, Martin CE (1948) Sexual Behaviour in the Human Male. Philadelphia, PA: Saunders.

Kinsey AC, Pomeroy WB, Martin CE et al. (1953) Sexual Behaviour in the Human Female. Philadelphia, PA: Saunders.

Kirby RS (1996) Recent advances in the medical management of prostate cancer. British Journal of Clinical Practice 50(5): 287.

Koo MB (2001) Erotized transference in the male patient–female therapist dyad. Journal of Psychotherapy Practice & Research 10(1): 28–36.

Ladas AK, Whipple B, Perry J (1982) The G-Spot and Other Discoveries about Sexuality. New York: Holt, Rinehart & Winston.

Laumann EO, Gagnon JH, Michael RT et al. (1994) The Social Organisation of Sexuality: Sexual Practices in the United States. Chicago: University of Chicago Press.

Lee JA (1973) The Colours of Love: An Exploration in the Ways of Loving. Ontario: New Press.

Leif HI (1988) Foreword. In Leiblum SR, Rosen RC (eds.), Sexual Desire Disorders. New York: Guilford Press.

LeVay S (1991) A difference in hypothalamic structure between heterosexual and homosexual men. Science 253(5023): 1034–1037.

Lightfoot-Klein MA (1989) The sexual experience and marital adjustment of genitally circumcised and infibulated females in the Sudan. Journal of Sex Research 26(3): 375–392.

Loulan J (1984) Lesbian Sex. Minneapolis: Spinsters Ink.

Love B (1992) The Encyclopaedia of Unusual Sexual Practices. London: Abacus Books.

Lunde DT, Morgan J (1980) The Die Song: A Journey into the Mind of a Mass Murderer. New York: W. W. Norton.

Margolis J (2004) O: The Intimate History of the Orgasm. London: Random House.

Masters WH, Johnson VE (1966) Human Sexual Response. Boston: Little, Brown.

McWhirter DP, Mattison AM (1984) The Male Couple: How Relationships Develop. Englewood Cliffs, NJ: Prentice-Hall.

Meloy JR (1992) The Psychopathic Mind: Origins, Dynamics and Treatment. Northvale, NJ: Jason Aronson Inc.

Meloy JR (1998) The psychology of stalking. In Meloy JR (ed.), The Psychology of Stalking: Clinical and Forensic Perspectives. London: Academic Press.

Milton M, Coyle A (1999) Lesbian and gay affirmative psychotherapy: issues in theory and practice. Sexual and Marital Therapy 14(1): 43–59.

Money J (1986) Lovemaps: Clinical Concepts of Sexual/Erotic Health and Pathology, Paraphilia, and Gender Transposition in Childhood, Adolescence, and Maturity. Amherst, New York: Prometheus Books.

Money J, Tucker P (1975) Sexual Signatures: On Being a Man or a Woman. Boston: Little, Brown.

Money JE (1972) Man and Woman, Boy and Girl. Baltimore, MD: Johns Hopkins University Press.

Moore SL, May M (1982) Satyriasis from a contemporary perspective: a review of hypersexuality. Hillside Journal of Clinical Psychiatry 4: 83–93.

Morin J (1998) Anal Pleasure Health. A Guide for Men & Women (3rd edn.) San Francisco, CA: Down There Press.

Mosner C (1992) A response to Aviel Goodman's 'Sexual addiction: designation and treatment'. Journal of Sex & Marital Therapy 19(3): 220–224.

Moynihan R (2003) The making of a disease: female sexual dysfunction. British Medical Journal 326: 45–47.

Mustanski BS, Bailey JM (2003) A therapist's guide to the genetics of human sexual orientation. Sexual and Relationship Therapy 18(4): 429–436.

Nadig P (1986) Utility of the vacuum–constriction device for men who have failed erectile prostheses. Journal of Urology Part 2(135): 232A.

Ng EML (2000) Towards a bio-psychosocial model of vaginismus: response to Janice Hiller. Sexual and Relationship Therapy 15(1): 91.

O'Keefe M, Hunt DK (1985) Assessment and the treatment of impotence. Medical Clinician of North America 79: 415–434.

Ogrodniczuk JS, Piper WE, McCallum M (2001) Effect of patient gender on outcome in two forms of short-term individual psychotherapy. Journal of Psychotherapy Practice & Research 10(2): 69–78.

Pacey S (2004) Couples and the first baby: responding to new parents' sexual and relationship problems. Sexual and Marital Therapy 19(3): 223–246.

Pattatucci AML, Hamer DH (1995) The genetics of sexual orientation: From fruit flies to humans. In Abramson PR, Pinkerton SD (eds.), Sexual Nature Sexual Culture. London: University of Chicago Press.

Pauly I (1974) Female transsexualism I and II. Archives of Sexual Behaviour 3(6): 487–526.

Person ES, Hagelin A, Fonagy P (1993) On Freud's 'Observations of Transference-Love'. New Haven, CT: Yale University Press.

Peterson JR (1983) The Playboy readers' sex survey, Part 1. Playboy 30: 108.

Pfeiffer E (1974) Sexuality in the aging individual. Journal of the American Geriatrics Society 22(11): 481–484.

Quadland MC (1985) Compulsive sexual behaviour: definition of a problem and an approach to treatment. Journal of Sex & Marital Therapy 11(2): 121–132.

Rappaport EA (1956) The management of an eroticized transference. Psychoanalytic Quarterly 25: 515–529.

Rhodes JC, Kjerulff KH, Lamgenberg PW et al. (1999) Hysterectomy and sexual functioning. Journal of the American Medical Association 282(20): 1934–1941.

Riley AJ (1988) The endocrinology of sexual function and dysfunction. In Cole M, Dryden W (eds.), Sex Therapy in Britain. Milton Keynes: Open University Press.

Riley AJ (1998) Sexual Drive Disorders. Paper presented at the Recent Advances in the Management of Common Sexual Disorders Conference, Birmingham.

Rinehart NJ, McCabe MP (1997) Hypersexuality: psychopathology or normal variant of sexuality. Sexual and Marital Therapy 12(1): 45–60.

Robson KM, Brant HA, Kumar R (1981) Maternal sexuality during first pregnancy and after childbirth. British Journal of Obstetrics and Gynaecology 88(9): 882–889.

Rose C (2002) Talking gender but who's listening? Counselling & Psychotherapy Journal August(13): 6–9.

Rosen RC, Rosen LR (1981) Human Sexuality. New York: Alfred Knopf.

Ross MW, Kauth MR (2002) Men who have sex with men, and the Internet: Emerging clinical issues and their management. Cooper A (ed.), Sex and the Internet. A Guidebook for Clinicians (pp. 47–70). New York: Brunner-Routledge.

Rowe RJ (1997) Bert & Lori: The Autobiography of a Crossdresser. New York: Prometheus Books.

Rueben D (1969) Everything You Wanted to Know About Sex But Were Afraid to Ask. New York: McKay.

Schlegel A (1995) The cultural management of adolescent sexuality. In Abramson PR, Pinkerton SD (eds.), Sexual Nature Sexual Culture (pp. 177–194). London: University of Chicago Press.

Schnarch DM (1991) Constructing the Sexual Crucible: An Integration of Sexual and Marital Therapy. New York: W. W. Norton.

Schneider JP (1994) Sexual addiction: Controversy within mainstream addiction medicine, diagnosis based on the DSM-III-R and physician case histories. Sexual Addiction and Compulsivity 1(1): 19–44.

Schneider JP (2000) A qualitative study of cybersex participants, gender differences, recovery issues, and implications for therapists. Sexual Addiction and Compulsivity 7(4): 250–278.

Schore A (1994) Affect Regulation and the Development of the Self. New Jersey: Lawrence Erlbaum.

Singer B, Kancelbaum B, Thomas R (2004) Men and women in therapy 2004: Inside the gender gap: New Harris Interactive Survey.

Smith CLB (1978) Maternal behaviour and perceived sex of infant revisited. Child Development 49: 1263–1265.

Sonnex C (1996) A General Practitioner's Guide to Genitourinary Medicine and Sexual Health. Cambridge: Cambridge University Press.

Starr BD, Weiner MB (1981) The Starr-Weiner Report on Sex and Sexuality in the Mature Years. New York: McGraw Hill.

Struve J (1990) Dancing with the patriarchy: the politics of sexual abuse. In Hunter M (ed.), The Sexually Abused Male. Prevalence, Impact and Treatment (Vol. 1: 3–46) Lexington, MA: Lexington Books.

Taleporos G, McCabe MP (2003) Relationships, sexuality and adjustment among people with physical disability. Sexual and Relationship Therapy 18(1): 25–44.

Tennot D (1979) Love and Limerance. The Experience of Being in Love. New York: Stein and Day.

Tiger L (1992) The Pursuit of Pleasure. New York: Little, Brown.

Tollison CD, Adams HE (1979) Sexual Disorders. New York: Garner Press.

Walster EH, Walster GW (1978) A New Look at Love. Reading, MA: Addison-Wesley.

Weller I (1995) AIDS. In Adler MW (ed.), ABC of Sexually Transmitted Diseases. London: BMJ Publishing Group.

Wilson RA, Wilson TA (1963) The fate of non-treated menopausal women: A plea for the maintenance of adequate oestrogen from puberty to the grave. Journal of American Geriatric Society 11: 352–356.

Winnicott DW (1960) The theory of parent–infant relationship. International Journal of Psycho-Analysis 41(Nov–Dec): 585–595.

Witherow R (1996) Surgical management of erectile dysfunction. International Journal of STD & AIDS July (suppl. 3): 19–21.

Zandvliet T (2000) Transgender Issues in Therapy. In Davies CND (ed.), Issues in Therapy with Lesbian, Gay, Bisexual and Transgender Clients. Buckingham: Open University Press.

Index

Sexual Offences Act 2003, 20, 22–23,
    107–108
sex offenders 113
sexual orientation, 8–9, 10, 11, 41
sexual phobia, 13, 70
sexual positions, 4
sexual reassignment surgery (SRS), 19,
    95–99, 103
Singer B, 81, 131
Sonnex C, 31, 131
Spencer A, 11, 128
spina bifida, 57
sildenafil, 1–2
Smith CLB, 11, 131
Starr BD, 27, 131
Steiner BW, 94, 126
sterilization, 76–77, 122
stigmatophilia, 117
Strong D, 71, 72, 91, 125
Struve J, 89, 131

Taleporos G, 32, 131
tampons, 36, 37
tantric sex, 59
Taylor SE, 8, 127
telephonicophilia, 112, 117
Tennot D, 56, 131
termination of pregnancy, 38, 74
testes, 16
testosterone, 16, 27, 42, 44, 46, 53,
    97–98, 100
testicular feminising syndrome, 101
Thomas R, 81, 131
Tiger L, 120, 131
Tollison CD, 89, 131
transference, 5
    erotic, 81–86, 121
    eroticised, 82, 121
transgenderist, 7, 88, 93–95, 122
transsexual, 93–95, 122
transvestic fetishism, 94
transvestite, 93–95, 117
tuberculosis, 68
Tucker P, 19, 130
Turner syndrome, 100
type T personality, 71

undervirilized, 16
Uprima, 55
urophilia, 113, 117
U-spot, 4, 40

vaccum pump, 55
vaginal
    atrophy, 27, 42, 46
    dryness, see vaginal lubrication
    lubrication, 39, 41, 42, 46, 48
vaginismus, 35, 37–38, 41
vaginitis, 41
vaginoplasty, 47, 97, 100, 122
vascular degeneration, 27
vasectomy, 73–74, 76, 122
Viagra, 1–2, 34, 51–52, 55–56
vibrator, see sex aid
virilization, 17, 122
voyeurism, 112, 117
Vukadinovic Z, 68, 125
vulva, 36
vulvar vestibulitis, 41

Walster EH, 12, 131
Walster GW, 12, 131
Weiner WB, 27, 131
Weller I, 31, 131
Whipple B, 24, 129
Wilson K, 78, 128
Wilson RA, 45, 131
Wilson TA, 45, 131
Winnicott DW, 66, 132
Witherow R, 63, 131
Wylie K, 81, 127

X-spot, 4, 40

Yohimbine, 55

Zandvliet T, 7, 132
zoophilia, 112, 117